THE
SPORTSMAN

THE
SPORTSMAN

Unexpected Lessons from an
Around-the-World Sports Odyssey

DHANI JONES
with Jonathan Grotenstein

RODALE.

Book design by Scott Russo

Library of Congress Cataloging-in-Publication Data
Jones, Dhani.
  The sportsman : unexpected lessons from an around-the-world sports odyssey / Dhani Jones, Jonathan Grotenstein.
      p.   cm.
  ISBN 978-1-60961-111-8 hardback
  1. Jones, Dhani—Travel.   2. Football players—United States.   3. Sports—Anecdotes.
4. Travel—Anecdotes.   I. Grotenstein, Jonathan.   II. Title.
GV939.J635A3   2011
796.332092—dc22
  [B]   2011010304

Distributed to the trade by Macmillan
2   4   6   8   10   9   7   5   3   1   hardcover

We inspire and enable people to improve their lives and the world around them.
www.rodalebooks.com

"Twenty years from now you will be more disappointed by the things that you didn't do than by the ones you did do. So throw off the bowlines. Sail away from the safe harbor. Catch the trade winds in your sails. Explore. Dream. Discover."

—Mark Twain

Contents

Part Two: Tackling the Globe

Introduction

The man sitting across from me is *bleeding*. The blood is pouring from his nose and leaking out of his eyes. Both of his orbital sockets have been fractured, causing his face to cave in like it was made of wet cardboard. It's going to take emergency surgery to restore it. I'm not sure "restore" is even the right word. There's no way his face is ever going to look the same.

The man isn't a stranger. We've been training together for a week here in Phnom Penh, where I'm learning *pradal serey,* an ancient Cambodian form of kickboxing. Each day our teacher, or *kruu,* Long Salavorn, has led us through a battery of drills and exercises in preparation for an actual fight against a real opponent.

Another man sitting next to me has just finished his. He's been training for a lot longer than a week.

I don't know where my kruu is right now. No one seems able to explain his absence, at least not in English. A trainer I have never met before is rubbing a mysterious oil into my shoulders. When he finishes, he clears his throat and spits on my back.

"For good luck," he insists.

A kid, also a stranger, is wrapping my hands with tape. He's nervous, and it's not at all clear to me that he knows what he's doing. A million thoughts are running through my head, not the least of which is *Why?*

Then it's time to put those thoughts away. It's my turn to get into the ring.

The Sportsman

There was a time, not that long ago, when a certain kind of man, usually—let's be honest—a very rich and very white man, would test his mettle on safari. Armed with a gun, his wits, and maybe a local guide to get him from here to there, he travelled into the wilderness on the hunt for dangerous prey. Afterward, he could share his stories with the fellows at the lodge or decorate his game room with stuffed heads and elephant tusks.

You'd call that man a sportsman.

For the sportsman, killing the beast was only a small part of the experience. The hunt was also about feeling a heightened sense of adrenaline. Facing his fears. Getting outside his comfort zone. He might even connect with his prey in a way that taught him something new about himself. While his focus couldn't have been narrower—find and kill the target—the activity itself opened up a whole new world of ideas and emotions.

I don't own a gun, and I've never killed anything larger than a fly. But that doesn't mean I haven't wanted to. The same impulses and emotions that fueled the sportsman flow through my mind and body when I'm pursuing a running back, shredding a fresh layer of snow, or competing in a sport that, a week earlier, was completely unfamiliar to me. The thrill of the hunt never lasts for long, but its lessons do—strengthening my body, mind, and soul.

———

Nobody lives forever. Nowhere is that more evident than in the NFL. Forget National Football League—most players will tell you it really stands for Not For Long. The average career doesn't last 4 years.

I just finished my 11th season. I'm a middle linebacker, not just a starter but defensive captain of the Cincinnati Bengals, having led the team in tackles for each of the past four seasons.

Four seasons ago, football gave every indication of being done with me. I was cut by both the Philadelphia Eagles and the New Orleans Saints, and none of the nibbles from other squads seemed to be panning out. While other players were studying playbooks and dreaming about the Super Bowl, I was staring at the Pacific Ocean, trying to figure out what I was going to do with the rest of my life. Maybe it would be public speaking, or a job with one of the networks. I could devote more time to my business interests, like the bow tie and advertising companies I'd started, or to my growing interest in photography. Hell, Hollywood was only an hour north—maybe I'd become an actor.

Instead I got a call from the Bengals, and when a few injuries created an opportunity for me, I suddenly found myself with a starting job. Even more surprising was how prepared I was—physically, mentally, spiritually—to step into the role, a reinvention and rebirth of my career.

I have to credit my off-season.

For some players, the off-season means rest and relaxation. A more dedicated player might hire a personal trainer, start a new workout regimen, or change his diet.

For me, the off-season means playing rugby in London, cricket in Jamaica, and jai alai in the Basque country of Spain. I've had dozens of fights: Muay Thai boxing in Bangkok, *lutte* wrestling in Senegal, and *schwingen* in Switzerland. I've raced bicycles up the mind-numbingly steep Italian Alps and dragon boats through the canals and quays of Singapore. I've practiced *sambo* in Russia and the ancient art of pradal serey in Cambodia. I've even climbed most of the way up Mount Everest.

Since we're being honest, I can tell you that I didn't do these things as part of some grand scheme to extend my career; I did them for a TV show. *Dhani Tackles the Globe.* The premise was pretty simple: I'd travel to a place, spend a week learning a local sport (and, since it was for the Travel Channel, explore the culture, customs, and cuisine), then compete against some of the native residents.

But what does it mean to "tackle the globe"? To grab hold of it and wrestle it into submission? That's what I thought, at first anyway. Me against the world. You want to compete? Bring it on. Throw your worst at me; I'll just turn on my apeshit switch and knock you back with something stronger.

Only a very strange thing happened along the way: I discovered that I was cross-training in ways I never would have imagined.

I became physically stronger, carrying 300-pound rocks in Iceland and grinding sails off New Zealand. I increased my mental toughness by crashing skulls with rugby players in England and by pushing myself to ride up a 10 percent grade for 20 miles during a 100-mile bicycle race in Italy. I learned about honor and tradition while hurling in Ireland, and how the Thai use their age-old style of kickboxing to balance the warrior spirit with the sage. Experiencing the close-knit connection among the Basque helped me to reignite my own passion for family and friends; a trip to Senegal allowed me to reconnect with my ancestry. I've overcome language, economic, and racial barriers to build camaraderie with hundreds of people whose lives are radically different from my own, communicating through humanity's most primal and universal language— competition.

As I started to compete with everyone, I discovered that it wasn't just about beating the other guy, but about connecting in a way that allowed me to learn something about myself. The world might try its hardest to kick my ass, serving up black eyes, busted lips, and the occasional fall from a horse, but it wasn't trying to take me out.

The world wanted to be my teacher, as long as I was willing to pay attention to the lessons.

A week is not a long time to spend in a place. Engaging with new people and places through competition, however, can be a kind of shortcut, slicing through language and cultural and social differences to find the common denominators that make us human.

My father likes to say that the world is just a house with many rooms. But it's also a gymnasium, a school, a restaurant, and a psychiatrist's couch. It has allowed me to unlock aspects of my body, mind, and spirit that had previously been unknown to me.

The larger and more complicated the world became, the simpler I became to myself.

I became a better football player. But I like to think that I also became a better person. I unlocked my inner sportsman, not in the stuffy old-white-guy-killing-animals kind of way, but as a responsible global citizen who used the power of the world to empower himself. To overcome stereotypes and expectations. To deepen his sense of independence while strengthening the bonds with the people around him. To redefine the possible.

You can do it, too. The sportsman exists inside each and every one of us, and he's waiting to come out and play.

PART ONE

Laying Tracks

Dhani Makalani
(Potomac)

My parents took 2 weeks to name me. They wanted to figure out who I was before locking it down. Per the wishes of Commander Samuel L. Jones, U.S. Navy (Ret.)—a.k.a. Dad—my name also had to satisfy three requirements.

(1) It would call me to purpose, demanding some action from me.

(2) It would honor my ethnicity, which, according to my father, was an African American spirit with a Eurocentric mind.

(3) It couldn't be shortened into a nickname.

My parents finally settled on Dhani (Hindi for "thinking man") Makalani (Hawaiian for "skilled at writing"). And while I tried for years to find a nickname—everything from "D.J." to "Oscar the Grouch"—my father is satisfied that his mission was a success.

———

I didn't play a down of football until high school. My mother didn't let me. Thought the game was too violent. She was an anesthesiologist, so she knew something about pain and injury. I gave her the benefit of the doubt.

So instead of playing football as a kid, I played every other sport.

I swam and raced mountain bikes. I played competitive tennis and wrestled. There were baseball, soccer, and basketball teams. I messed around with lacrosse and hockey on in-line skates. In the summers I'd canoe and kayak; when it got cold, I'd go snowboarding.

I played for fun, but for as long as I can remember, I played to win. You'll often hear people talk about someone having a "competitive nature." I am that someone. Winning was always in the front of my mind. The only option. Whatever I did, I wanted to be first.

It's like being in a classroom. You sit in the back, and you'll see a big room with a lot of people. Intimidating. Easy to get lost.

Sit in the center if you like being caught up in the middle of the pack. But who wants to be in the middle of the pack?

I want to be in the front row, where it's just the professor and me. That's where I can focus, unfiltered, on whatever it is I'm supposed to be learning.

———

I was also born with the proverbial chip on my shoulder. For as long as I can remember, I've been arguing with just about everyone: friends, teachers, coaches, my parents. I was also blessed (or cursed, depending on your point of view) with a sharp tongue. I set an elementary school record for trips to the principal's office.

Sometimes I was just being a brat, acting out. Like when I told my swim coach I wouldn't get into the water. Too damn cold. I knew he couldn't do anything to me, not really: I was the one who was going to win all the events come Saturday.

But I like to think it wasn't always about immaturity. Sometimes I was taking a stand, arguing for something I believed in. Like when I got into it with the middle school teacher who didn't believe that I'd completed my project on time travel without help. I was really into time travel, a young Albert Einstein, for all I knew. I fully expected that my efforts were going to be celebrated for their obvious genius.

When the teacher had the audacity to question those efforts, I think I told her to kindly suck my left nut. Or maybe that was the time I argued with my track coach. Who cares? You get the idea.

Point is, there's no way to say that kindly.

Another trip to the principal's office.

What frustrated me the most was that the teachers and coaches weren't looking at me the way one person looks at another person— they were looking at me the way 40-year-old adults look at 13-year-old kids. I am all for respecting one's elders, but I was sure, even then, that if I had some pertinent information, backed up and well justified, I should be able to say it. Just because you've been through *something* doesn't mean that you know *everything*. That's the whole point behind that show, *Are You Smarter Than a 5th Grader?*

Little mofos know some shit.

Anyway, I wasn't always an easy kid. My mother once kicked me out of the car for lipping off. Told me to walk home. Fifteen miles away. My father, a Navy captain who'd seen and dealt with much tougher cases than mine, had more of a "buck stops here" policy. He told me, when I was 13, that if I continued down the path I was travelling, I'd be dead by 18. Maybe at his own hands. As far as he was concerned, he brought me into the world—and he could take me out. Didn't stop me from arguing, but at least taught me to be a little more strategic with my words.

A NOTE FROM COMMANDER SAMUEL L. JONES (A.K.A. DAD)

There is a saying that I like to use: "Sow a thought, and you reap an act; Sow an act, and you reap a habit; Sow a habit, and you reap a character; Sow a character, and you reap a destiny."

Dhani was running around with a group of young men who, in my eyes, lacked sufficient character. Now, two things came out of this. The first was a big hole in my basement wall. A Dhani-size hole. The second was that he quickly moved away from that group. But I didn't try to tell Dhani to move away from them; I engaged those young men in a way that moved them away from Dhani.

I challenged them in their own lives. I got in their faces and stayed with them, letting them see that they couldn't stay up with me, they couldn't match me, and they weren't going to have any influence on this son of mine because I was going to be right there in their Kool-Aid. I gave them a choice: Either they come the way we want to go, or they go away.

But I never tried to force or otherwise convince Dhani to choose between me and his friends. Because another saying that I use is "What you do speaks so loudly that what you say I cannot hear."

I grew up in Potomac, Maryland, one of maybe five black kids in a predominantly Jewish neighborhood. I knew how to do the Hava Nagila long before I knew the steps to the Humpty Dance.

Potomac was a welcoming place, relatively free of racism, at least in any overt way. There were a few subtle things now and then, like a teacher who told me to take my "cotton-pickin' hands" off something or another. The Congressional Country Club, where I played a lot of tennis, wasn't exactly integrated when I was a kid, and there were certain line judges who made calls against me that left me feeling suspicious.

But mostly I felt welcomed. My parents were both world travellers—my mother caught the bug after a college year abroad in Africa, while my father's naval career took him to Japan and the Philippines—and as soon as my sister and I were old enough, they began taking us with them. The international flavor didn't end when we got home. Mom's best friend was Egyptian; my parents had friends from Russia, India, Pakistan, Ghana, Kenya, Ethiopia, and Jamaica.

This felt natural to me. It didn't even feel like being an outsider, just the completely normal experience of a young man looking for his place in society.

A young man with a huge chip on his shoulder.

━━━━━━━

By the time I reached high school, that chip was more like a log. Everybody was pretty sick of arguing with me. My father encouraged my mother to let me make more of my own decisions, so I could learn to live with the consequences. One of the first was to go out for the football team.

Consequences there were. I hated it. Autumn in Potomac was hot and muggy. Two-a-day practices sucked. I felt like I was being taught how to steer a car at full speed into a brick wall, then being told to enjoy it. Every practice I got my ass beat, my body pounded into the ground. Every day there was someone to drive me back 60 yards, put me on my back, and step on me on his way off the field. I was definitely sitting in the back of the classroom.

Was I frustrated? Hell yes. I was dealing with people who were better than me. There were fights. But the experience helped to motivate me. I wasn't the king of the world anymore. I had to look at my teammates, every practice, and say, "You know what? You guys got a lot on me right now."

One part of my brain told me I could quit, that I had too many other things to do with my life. But my subconscious mind was building a rock-solid foundation. *If you're going to do this,* it told me, *these are the hurdles you have to climb.* This may not have been the experience I expected when I signed up, but I'd signed up. I'd made a commitment to football, and I was too proud, too stubborn, and too competitive to admit I'd made a mistake.

Fortunately, football paid an immediate dividend: The game turned out to be the perfect antidote to the chip on my shoulder. When

I got home after two practices, all I wanted to do was my homework so I could go to bed. I was too damn tired to argue. It felt good not to have to argue anymore.

There's a conference table in my mind. Eight guys, maybe more. One's drinking coffee, one's drinking tea, one's drinking orange juice. Others have scotch, gin, or vodka, maybe a gimlet. One guy is happy with a glass of water.

They're all dressed differently. Bow ties and neckties. A ratty T-shirt and a pinstripe suit from the 1930s. Slacks and shorts. Woolworth's and Ralph Lauren. One is butt-ass naked.

Who am I? I'm the moderator of this roundtable discussion. It's my job to make sure that all these characters accept one another for who they are. I've got to mediate arguments and make sure that everyone's drink is kept full. Sometimes extra full: No one's too upset when the Angry Guy gets so drunk he passes out in the corner.

Sometimes I'll let one of these characters take the lead. There's a very different guy, say, meeting with a TV executive than there is when I'm on the football field. But mostly I just try to keep them all on the same page. I'm a Pisces: As long as the fish are swimming in the same direction, things will go well.

But when they start fighting, it can really mess me up.

I remember one time, just walking down the street, I got to a corner and didn't know which way to go.

So I sat there.

For 3 hours.

Finally, it got late and I got hungry. Then it was time to go eat.

I played fullback and defense, at least until the coaches got to see my hands. I had terrible hands. They told me to concentrate on defense, where my hands wouldn't be a liability. The move also made my mother much happier—she felt a lot better when I was tackling people instead of the other way around.

I got better at finding the fun within the game, eventually learning to enjoy it. Football started to mean a lot to me. But it never meant *everything* to me. I had too many other things going on.

My junior year in high school, I was still competing in swim meets, tennis matches, and mountain bike races. I was a varsity wrestler and lettered in track. I still went snowboarding whenever I could. I entered triathlons and went on white-water rafting trips.

I played saxophone in the school band, performing at football games until I made varsity and the coaches asked me to quit. I kind of wish I hadn't—it would have been cool to come out at halftime, in pads, to get down with the band.

I had school projects. I raised money for muscular dystrophy. I had a social life. On top of it all, I had a full load of AP classes. Sports were my avocation, not my vocation: I was going to be a doctor.

It was a dream that started when I was a kid, bragging about all the things that I was going to do with my life. My father told me plainly that if I wanted to do all those things, I was going to have to find a job that paid a lot of money. That afternoon, after some quick research into potential careers and their expected salaries, I hung a sign on my bedroom door: Dr. Dhani Jones, Pediatric Neurosurgeon.

Let's just say there weren't too many other football players discussing their AP biology exams during practice.

My coaches worried that all my activities were going to distract me from football. Pretty much everyone else thought I was crazy, that I should slow down. Life shouldn't be that chaotic.

But for me, the chaos was part of the routine, as long as I stayed focused on the task at hand. When I was playing football, I was concentrating on football. When I was in class, I was concentrating on class. Being busy didn't make me scattered—it helped me to focus better on whatever activity I happened to be participating in.

More importantly, my *performance* got better in everything I did.

Football workouts are about three things: getting faster, getting stronger, and getting more explosive. That meant a lot of running, lifting, and slamming my body into blocking sleds. But the benefits extended beyond the football field. All that running made me better at track. The lifting made me a more formidable wrestler and an absolute beast when I was pedaling a mountain bike up a hill. The explosiveness allowed me to close faster to the net and hit the ball harder, helping me to win more tennis matches.

It wasn't a one-way relationship: The other sports helped me to become a better football player. Tennis forced me to practice my lateral movement, hand-eye coordination, and quickness. Track and biking improved my aerobic fitness. I could play football faster and for longer stretches without getting tired and with greater agility.

In the end, all those "distractions" helped me go from a practice scrub to the guy getting his name in the paper: All-County, All-Met, and one of the top-rated linebacker prospects on the East Coast.

Be the Outlier

My mother warned me that football was a violent game. She wasn't wrong. I remember suffering my first concussion during the first half of a game my junior year. The next thing I remember is getting pizza after the game. As the middle linebacker, it was my job to call out the defensive plays on the field. My teammates told me later that I'd made quite a few strange calls during the second half.

The summer between my junior and senior years, I developed a limp. I ignored it, figuring it would go away. My mother noticed it during a church-group basketball game, after the coach's wife pointed it out to her: "Dhani sure looks slow dribbling down the court. I thought he was a better athlete than that." After a few minutes of maternal defensiveness—"Well, you know, basketball isn't really his sport, and besides, he's probably reading the court or something like that . . ."—my mother's medical training kicked in. She started to suspect that there was something else wrong with me. When I couldn't keep up with her on a shopping trip a couple of weeks later, she was sure of it. We went to see the doctor.

I had a herniated disk in my back. I was going to need surgery. "How long will it take me to recover?" I asked. "Football starts in 2 weeks."

"Football?" the doctor replied, almost sounding surprised. "You're not going to play football again."

He showed me the statistics. Told me all the reasons why I probably couldn't and definitely shouldn't get back on the field.

In other words, he did the exact opposite of what he should have done.

I'm the person who, you tell me I shouldn't do something, you might as well have ordered me to go ahead and do it. Especially if it's something that I believe in.

I had the surgery, popped out of bed, and proceeded to pass out and collapse on the floor. Low blood pressure. I thought I was going to die.

A few days later, I had recovered enough to go back to the doctor for an evaluation. The surgery was a success, he told me, but I could still forget about football.

I didn't cuss him out, exactly, but I was pretty stern in my beliefs. Most of the people undergoing this surgery were in their 40s, 50s, and 60s. I reminded him that I didn't have the body of a middle-aged man; I was 17. There was no way in the world that he was going to tell me I couldn't play football because of the stats. I'm not a statistic. If anything, I'm the outlier.

I walked out of the room and began my rehab: lifting and running. Five weeks into the season, I felt like I was strong enough to play. This time we went to a different doctor, a guy in DC who had worked with the Redskins. He cleared me to play. My high school coach took a little more convincing. He finally let me back on the field—as the kicker. So I kicked off, punted, nailed a few extra points, and at the end of the game played a series at linebacker. By the next game I was starting again. We didn't lose another game until the state championship.

After my first year at Michigan, I went back to see the original doctor. I brought him a football, placed it on his desk, and quietly left the office.

"NSATIBL"
(Ann Arbor)

Football was supposed to be a stepping-stone, not a way of life. The game was a means of helping me to control my temper, funneling the energy that made me argue and battle with other people into something more productive, or better yet, dissolving it altogether. It certainly wasn't going to be the economic engine that fueled my future—that's what my education was for. My plan was to be a doctor.

But I made enough plays on the field for a few colleges to come calling. I had interest from schools ranging from Brown to the University of Washington. Maryland and Michigan had rolling admissions and accepted me on scholarship the summer before my senior year.

Then I had back surgery. As soon as the schools heard about my diskectomy, almost all the offers disappeared. Only the University of Washington was still willing to take a chance on me.

I had visited the campus the previous spring. I loved the way Seattle sat below Mount Rainier, beside the Pacific Ocean, right next to Canada. The hills were covered in purple flowers. Sure, it rained a little, but it was more of a misting than anything serious. The sky is always grey in Boston and no one has a problem going to college there.

But I had my heart set on the University of Michigan. It wasn't because it was the place where my parents met. It wasn't because, as a sophomore in high school, I'd seen them win the Holiday Bowl in San Diego, where—according to my mother—I'd stood up on my seat and screamed, "I can do it better!"

I wanted to go to Michigan because of a pamphlet I'd seen during my visit there. There was a picture of a globe with a giant letter *M* on top of it. *If I want to be on top of the world,* I thought, *I've got to go to Michigan.*

A NOTE FROM DR. NANCY JONES (A.K.A. MOM)

This was the time when [Michigan coach] Bo Schembechler had left, and his successor, Gary Moeller, had gotten into some kind of, I guess, disagreement *at a bar downtown, which led to him being relieved of his duty. And coach Lloyd Carr was appointed as interim head coach. Tim Biakabutuka, their running back, decided to leave school early, so they were all caught up in finding a replacement. They already had Jarrett Irons, who was everybody's everything in terms of linebacker, to the extent that he was on the cover of* Sports Illustrated. *Plus they had another linebacker named Grady Brooks whom they were recruiting.*

Well, to make a long story short, Michigan wasn't looking at linebackers. They had done their perusal of the Washington, DC, area. I guess Dhani was listed at 190 pounds, so he really wasn't of interest.

Coach Shepherd, Dhani's high school coach, called and railed into the staff there. I don't know which coach he talked to. But he called until he got one of the Michigan coaches, and he gave him a piece of his mind, basically saying, "What is wrong with you guys? You have a student who has already been accepted to your university. You don't have to worry about getting him in—he's already been admitted. Both of his parents are alums. And other universities want him. And you aren't even asking him to come for a visit? You all must be crazy."

Consequently, we got a call and Dhani was invited for a visit in January. My husband, Samuel, and I joined him. Our host was the quarterback coach. Now, if you have a quarterback coach hosting a linebacker, what does that tell you? They weren't really interested in Dhani; they were just doing this visit out of courtesy. So Dhani enjoys the weekend, and then we had our interview with the head coach.

"Yes, son, you know," Coach Carr said to us, "you came on our radar screen a bit late, and we hadn't really been looking for linebackers, and you know, we don't really have any scholarship monies left. And, son, what's your interest in Michigan anyway?"

"Coach Carr," Dhani said, "I always wanted to wear the winged helmet," referring to the distinctive yellow design on Michigan's headgear.

"Well, son, when you come to Michigan, maybe what you can do is, you can be a walk-on on the team. And maybe next year we can find that scholarship money."

So that was the end of the interview. And as we stood up to leave, I said to Coach Carr, "I am very sorry, but I will not be paying $30,000 for my son to come and be a walk-on on this team. To make millions of dollars for this program. So if you don't have scholarship money for him now, no problem. Because he can go to the University of Washington, where they appreciate him. And seem to have the finances for him. But I want you to just be aware that when it comes to the Rose Bowl, you need to watch out for when Dhani will be sacking your quarterback. Thanks very much!"

Signing Day was coming up in 4 weeks. But 2 days after we got home, we got a call from Michigan's linebacker coach. He wants to come to Potomac on Wednesday to see Dhani up close. After he visits, Coach Carr calls. And he comes, like, 2 days later and offers Dhani a scholarship. I think that after

I challenged him, he said, "Maybe I need to look at this kid's film." And he saw the potential.

We thanked Coach Carr for visiting and told him that we thought the offer was great. "But Dhani will not live on South Quad with the rest of the athletes," I told him. "He needs to live at the Residential College, because he needs to pursue his intellectual pursuits."

Coach Carr said later that it was the first time he ever had a football player live outside the team's dorm. He went to visit the Residential College for the first time, to see what it was all about, before he agreed to do it. "I don't know why no one has ever asked me to do this," he told me. "Because it's not a total football experience. They're going to school to learn."

When you accept an athletic scholarship, you are there at the mercy of the coaches. You have to follow their rules, or else no more scholarship. It's kind of like your first contractual obligation: You're contracted to play football; they're contracted to educate you. But I knew it was a great opportunity. I'd have to be crazy to get kicked off the team.

Especially during the very first meeting.

The freshmen were called "YAPs"—young ass punks. They were expected to know their place in the chain, which was at the very bottom. There were all kinds of things YAPs weren't allowed to do, one of them being speaking at a team meeting.

The team captains stood in the front of the room, announcing that our team motto, our goal for the season, was going to be "Together."

So I raised my hand.

I saw Coach Carr, sitting in front of me, glance over his shoulder. He ignored my hand, so I kept it raised. The situation was quickly becoming uncomfortable. Finally, Coach turned around in his seat and asked, "What is it, Dhani?!"

"How are we going to be 'together' if we can't even talk?"

Coach Carr called me into his office after the meeting. "If you don't want to abide by the rules and what we're doing here, then we're going to have to let you go and take away your scholarship."

Day 1, causing problems. But maybe I was also creating solutions. It wasn't too long after that that the rule about YAPs was changed. Today, all the young people speak.

In many ways, college football forced me to narrow my focus. Drills didn't start "around 7:30"; they began precisely at 7:14 or 8:52. I was going to have to concentrate on a whole different level if I was going to survive. So I looked for ways to minimize distractions.

One of the first things I decided to do was to wear a uniform both on and off the field. I began wearing the same thing every day: gray sweatpants and a black-and-orange jacket so bright that it was almost impossible to sneak back to my dorm at 6:30 in the morning. (Almost.) I once went through a stretch where I wore the same shirt and pants for a month straight. Changed my underwear, but that was all.

It's a habit that has stayed with me. I don't wear the same clothes every day, but I almost always wear the same basic uniform: blue or grey jeans and a T-shirt, usually black.

Some people wake up in the morning and spend 20 minutes in the closet trying to figure out what to wear. Maybe you're that kind of person. I don't have anything against looking good or being fashionable. It's just that once you become the guy or girl who changes outfits *all the time*, people are going to expect that from you *all the time*. Why do you want to have that high level of expectation? Do you really want to wake up every morning and spend 20 minutes thinking, *Did someone see me in that yesterday?* Or do you just want people to look at you, nod, and say, "That's just what he wears."

Unless I'm dressing up, I don't want to be noticed for my clothes. I want people to focus on my words, posture, and body language.

The first person I noticed taking this minimalist approach to clothes was Steve Jobs. He supposedly got the idea from Albert Einstein. Steve Jobs has a billion dollars. Albert Einstein was a super-genius. I might as well take a page from those who know a little bit more than I do.

Besides, if you wear the same outfit all the time, then all of a sudden you change it up? People go, "Man, you got style."

So I had to narrow my focus. But I wasn't about to let it get too narrow.

I designed my own major, which I called "Self-Representation." I combined art classes, photography, painting, literature, and studies of the human body. My mother helped me keep track of all the biology and physiology classes I'd need to get into med school.

I joined the school newspaper as a photographer, taking pictures at basketball games, soccer matches, and gymnastics meets. I helped my friends Shomari Stone (now a television reporter in Washington) and Sean O'Neal (he's just a neurosurgeon) start one of the first student-created TV shows for the local university network. I did CD reviews, poetry readings, amateur kung fu, and a pretty good imitation of Shomari, who had already developed that reporter's voice.

Even though I had a scholarship, I took a part-time job at the local bike shop. I rode my bike everywhere. I wasn't about to give up snowboarding, either; we'd finish a game on Saturday, I'd hop in the car with Sean, and we'd drive to the mountain to shred the slopes under the lights.

I did my best to maintain a larger social perspective, as well. After hearing a lecture by Dr. Ben Carson, the brilliant pediatric neurosurgeon from Johns Hopkins, I was inspired to start a program called HEADS: Here Earning A Destiny with Honesty, Eagerness And Determination of Self. The idea was to create a forum for black men to communicate, to stop and say hello instead of just passing by one another with a "Whassup?" We gathered everybody from janitors to coaches, from the director of admissions to the head of the College of Literature, Science, and the Arts. We read books together, discussed what was going on in our lives, and staged the occasional campus protest.

I wanted to hang out with everybody. I liked the arts people, the intellectuals, the militants, and the international students who couldn't speak any language other than their own. I pledged Alpha Phi Alpha. As the only football player living in the residential dorm, I got to mix it up with everybody from transsexuals to homophobes. Premeds and prelaws. I grew out my hair and stopped combing it. I painted my toenails black.

To put it plainly, my license plate in college read "NSATIBL." Insatiable. I didn't just want to be a football player. I wanted to do everything.

Before you go getting too many ideas, you should also know that I was a late bloomer. I didn't have sex or an alcoholic beverage until my senior year of college. I'm not saying that I didn't party or do everything that a man and woman can do together except the deed itself, but I grew up in a Christian home where drink was a vice and sex was a blessed sacrament. I had ridiculous urges. I just didn't act on them.

Probably for the better.

Probably would have had some kids by now, if I did.

I'm enough kids to take care of.

When I had to focus on football, I focused on football.

First time I got on a scale, I weighed in at 207 pounds. The classic Michigan linebacker was supposed to be more like 240. Mike Gittleson, your prototypical old-school dinosaur/strength coach who had been there since the 1970s, called everybody over to the scale. "Hey you guys! Get over here! This kid over here thinks he can play linebacker at the University of Michigan." He embarrassed me in front of the whole room.

By now I was used to these kinds of challenges. I wasn't going to be strong enough. I wasn't going to be fast enough. I wasn't going to be big enough. I wasn't going to be able to do X, Y, and Z, which is why I was never going to succeed. Which is fine by me. That's how my life has always been. You can let it get you down, or you can use it as motivation to get better.

GITTLESON'S BOARDS

Mike Gittleson was a strength coach at Michigan for about 30 years. Old school. But in the 1980s, he'd been considered by many to be an innovator. His most famous invention—or infamous, if you happened to have played football at Michigan—was his "boards."

A board was basically a two-by-four, around 3 or 4 feet long. Three more pieces of wood, each about a foot long, were nailed into the bottom at equal intervals. The boards on the bottom created friction as we pushed the damn thing up and down the field for an hour. Might not seem so innovative today, but it was one hell of a workout.

I became a starter my sophomore year. We went undefeated, winning the Rose Bowl and the national championship. I finished second on the team in tackles and had six quarterback sacks and an interception. I also won the Frederick Matthaei Award for the junior-to-be "who has displayed leadership, drive, and achievement on the athletic field and in the classroom."

But I still didn't think that I was any good at football.

Compared to the rest of the team, maybe I wasn't. We had the Heisman Trophy winner, Charles Woodson, at cornerback. Almost half of the starting lineup made the All–Big Ten team, and 30 of my teammates would go on to the NFL—even the backup quarterback, a guy named Tom Brady.

I remember the moment the lightbulb went off for me. I was sitting in the linebacker room after a game, thinking about some of the plays I had made. That got me thinking about some of the plays I'd made in earlier games.

I had made a few plays.

Hell, I'd made a *shit-ton* of plays.

I turned to Eric Mayes, one of the team captains. "Man," I said, "I'm pretty good at this game, aren't I?"

"You're a baller," he said.

"I'm a baller," I repeated. "I'm a baller!"

Football: a game for humble men.

I called my mom to share the news. Told her there was even some talk that I might get drafted into the pros.

"That's nice, dear," she replied. "Just don't quit your day job."

―――――――――――

My senior year we went 10-2, finishing fifth in the country. We beat Alabama in overtime in the Orange Bowl. I stuffed Shaun Alexander, their star running back who was about to become an NFL first-round draft pick, two times behind the line of scrimmage.

I hadn't given up on medical school. My grades were good—I won the Dr. Arthur D. Robinson Award as the team's leading senior-scholar—and I planned to take the MCATs. But a few days before the draft, one of the coaches from the Dallas Cowboys flew to Potomac to take my mother and me out to dinner. He told me they wanted to pick me in the second round.

Maybe medical school could wait a couple of years.

Only the second round came and went. And all of a sudden it was the next day, and I was starting to doubt that I'd hear my name at all. It took until the sixth round—the second-to-last round of the draft—for me to get a call from the New York Giants.

I'd be lying if I said I wasn't disappointed. I looked back and tried to figure out what I could have done differently to put myself in a better position. But how long are you going to lament? How long are you going to wallow in your self-pity? After all, I had been drafted. I was going to play football.

Forget that. I wasn't just going to play—I was going to change the world's perception of the game. I was going to show everybody that a thinking man could be a football player, and that a football player could be a thinking man.

Looking the Part

I dedicated the summer to working out in the Giants' training facilities. One day as I entered the building, I was summoned to the front office. Ernie Accorsi, the team's general manager, wanted to talk to me.

I walked upstairs and knocked on the door, a little self-conscious in my jeans and T-shirt.

"Your contract is ready," Ernie said, pointing to the papers on the desk in front of him. "You ready to sign?"

"I don't intend any disrespect," I said, "but I'd prefer not to sign it today."

He looked confused. "Is something wrong? Is there a problem we need to discuss?"

"There's nothing wrong. If you don't mind, I'd just rather not do it today." I thanked him, changed into my sweats, and hit the treadmill.

The next day, I returned to the facility wearing a blue suit and red silk tie. "Mr. Accorsi," I said, "if it's okay with you, I'm ready to sign that contract now."

Yes, jeans and T-shirt are my uniform. But they're not my uniform for the football field. And they're not what I wear to conduct business.

When I finished signing the papers, I asked Ernie to take a picture of me that I could send to my parents.

Pitching Tents
and Tying Knots
(New York)

The knee is the largest and most complicated joint in the human body. It's the meeting place for three bones, including your two biggest—the femur and the tibia—whose job it is to support the entire weight of your body. The third bone, the patella, protects all the stuff going on inside the knee. And there's a lot of stuff to protect, because the knee isn't any simple hinge, but what physiologists call a mobile trocho-ginglymus, a hinge that not only bends, but also rotates.

The two big bones are separated by smooth and springy cartilage, which absorbs shock while allowing the knee to bend and rotate. The whole package is kept in place by a pair of crisscrossed ligaments, but one of them—the anterior cruciate ligament, or ACL—does almost all the work, keeping your femur attached to your tibia. Without the ACL, your tibia would constantly be flying around independently of your femur, which would not only look pretty weird, but also do severe damage to the cartilage every time you tried to push off your knee.

The Giants already had a solid group of linebackers, and, as a sixth-round pick, there was no guarantee I was going to make the roster. One of the first adages any rookie hears is that the three best ways to make a football team are "special teams, special teams, and special teams." If you're not going to be starting, then you had better damn well be ready to fly down the field on punts and kickoffs, throwing blocks and making tackles.

It can get pretty brutal out there, which is why most teams avoid using their starters on special teams in the first place. The caution even extended to practice: We'd often do kickoff drills at three-quarter speed without any real contact. Jog fast down the field, deliver an imaginary block, then cut to the side.

It was during one of these drills that I caught my cleat in the turf as I cut to the side. My knee twisted at a weird angle. I tumbled to the ground.

I picked myself up and limped over to the side of the field, figuring I'd sprained it. The trainers knew better. An MRI confirmed it: a torn ACL. Surgery, to be followed by rehabilitation. My first season in the pros was over before it had even begun.

When I woke up from the surgery, I found myself in the pediatric ward—I guess they were short on beds. So I lay there, listening to kids, thinking about what was ahead of me.

I tried to look at my life as a building. If I was going to get to the top, I was going to have to start with a foundation. But when my knee crumpled, my foundation crumbled, and it was going to be at least 6 months before I could think about rebuilding it.

If I couldn't build a foundation, maybe I could start with a tent. It's easy to build a tent—all you have to do is drive a few stakes in the ground. It might not be as strong as a building, but at least it would keep me dry while it rained. I would be sheltered until it was time to start rebuilding again.

So I started planting stakes in the ground wherever I could.

One of my first days with the Giants, I asked Michael Strahan, our All-Pro defensive end, what advice he had for getting by in the NFL.

"It's easy, man," Strahan said. "Smile, say please, and say thank you. It will get you in a lot of doors."

So I went to Peter John-Baptiste, the Giants' director of community relations, smiled, said please, and asked him what I could do to help the team.

Before too long, I was on a new mission nearly every day, going to speak at some event or talk to some group. High schools, middle schools, elementary schools. Boys' groups, girls' groups, DARE programs, Rotary clubs. I might speak to the Policemen's Athletic League one day, a roomful of death-row inmates the next. I wanted to improve my speaking skills and establish myself in the community. Plant those stakes in the ground.

I also started to see a different side of New York City. One event, a sort of celebrity auction, was sponsored by Toys"R"Us. I was excited when I got to meet the CEO, but even more amazed by the auction itself. Rosie O'Donnell was the host, presiding over bids that made my head spin. "Who will bid a million dollars? Come on, I'll bid a million if you bid a million. You know what? I'll do two if you do two. Let's bid four." I was starting to realize that New York was the type of place where, if you got to know the right people, you could really have an influential place in the world.

———

At night, I got to know the other side of New York. In other words, I partied my ass off.

I'm pretty sure I spent every dollar I made just as fast as I earned it. I think it happens to everybody when they get to New York City. Maybe if you're religiously devout or seriously involved with a partner to keep you out of trouble, you can avoid getting caught up by the pace. Or maybe you are so evolved as a person that you no longer feel the need to keep up with the proverbial Joneses.

But if you're young and single and have a few dollars in your pocket, you are going balls to the wall for the first year. The first 3 years. Maybe 10 years.

I like to think that it wasn't just mindless partying. All the social functions that I was involved in during the day kept me moving; they made sure I didn't become an alcoholic or a pothead. Not that I have anything against alcoholics or potheads—that's just not me.

When I went out at night, I tried to do so with a sense of purpose. Yes, I was having a good time. A damn good time. But I was also meeting all kinds of people from all different walks of life. It felt like everyone in New York City was doing something amazing in movies, music, the club industry, or Wall Street. Many of these people are still my friends today.

Hanging out with interesting people motivates you to pursue your own interests. I painted and took a lot of photos. I built a washboard bass and played for tips in the 42nd Street station—one day I made $4.85. I tried my hand at modeling, strutting with my headshots into the Wilhelmina agency. I got a summer internship in the sales and marketing department at the Loews Corporation and got really good at underlining things on pieces of paper.

I was planting stakes in the ground, building the shelter that would help me to rebuild my foundation.

The Bow Tie

"When you wear a bow tie, you
have to turn off the part of the
brain that cares about other
people's perceptions."

—TUCKER CARLSON

One summer during high school, I studied in an engineering program at Penn State University. That was where I met Kunta Littlejohn.

Kunta was the first guy I ever met who creased his pants. Didn't matter if he was sporting khakis or jeans; they'd always be immaculately laundered with a perfect crease down the middle. He ironed all his shirts, even the T-shirts. Everything about him was crisp, clean, and neatly pressed.

Except for his personality. Kunta was a big, jovial guy, larger than life, who always seemed to be laughing. I tend not to laugh that often, but I love hanging around with people who do.

In 2000, while I was recovering from my knee injury, Kunta was diagnosed with lymphoma. He was living in Philadelphia at the time, so when the Giants played the Eagles, I travelled with the team and spent the night at his house. He was as talkative as ever, just not about the cancer. Kunta wanted to talk about bow ties.

If you wanted to be somebody in the world, he told me, you've got to rock the bow tie.

I told him he was crazy. Nobody wore bow ties except for the Nation of Islam and Pee-wee Herman.

Kunta quickly corrected me. The bow tie, he explained, was the preferred style of dress among upstanding gentlemen—men who had conversations of substance about business, politics, and life's most important decisions. Senators used to wear bow ties. So did members of the press, back when news gathering was a little more, shall we say, genteel. A black-tie function was once considered the height of sophistication.

Kunta didn't care that people today associated the bow tie with Louis Farrakhan. Or Pee-wee Herman. He believed that it was an iconic article of fashion, one that still represented the essence of the Upstanding Gentleman. It was up to us to crush the new stereotypes, helping the bow tie to reestablish its old identity while maybe infusing it with something more modern.

Out of support for Kunta's battle against his illness—a battle, I'm happy to say, he eventually won—I decided that I would have to at least investigate his claims. When I got back to New Jersey, I went to the Paramus Park Mall, where the salesman at Nordstrom helped me pick out a bow tie and showed me the proper way to tie it.

The first time I wore the bow tie in a public setting, I was more than a little bit self-conscious. I knew people were going to ask me about it, that they would approach me with their own preconceptions about why I'd decided to wear one. If I wanted to flip their perceptions, I'd better damn well have a story, one that would leave them with an understanding that was different from "Are you a member of the Nation of Islam, a Republican, or just a big fan of Pee-wee Herman?"

"You know, it's funny you say that," I replied to the first person who asked me—and to everyone who has asked me since—"because before a lot of those people existed, there were a fair number of gentlemen who used to wear the bow tie. I wear one because I aspire to be an upstanding man of sophistication."

And then they look at me sideways. But they never think about the bow tie in the same way again.

A Good Vanilla Is a Great Ice Cream

When I go to my favorite restaurants, I always order the same thing. I like to have the same potato, the same cut of steak, the same dessert. I guess it's part of my therapy for myself.

Even after the Giants picked me, my mother had a hard time believing I was going to be a professional football player. "Just because you got drafted doesn't mean that they're going to give you a contract," she reminded me. Good old Mom, always with the dose of reality. So instead of standing by while I locked myself into a lease on a swank bachelor pad in the Village, or even corporate housing near the stadium, she found a friend who had a sister who would rent me a basement apartment in New Jersey for $1,000 a month.

The rent did not include access to the thermostat. I spent a lot of time being too hot or too cold.

At the start of my third year with the Giants, I figured it was time for me to have a place of my own. I bought a townhouse in Hackensack, a new construction that was nearly finished—I was going to get the chance to decorate the interior just the way I wanted it.

The exterior already had a pair of Julius Caesar columns with leaves wrapped around them, so I decided it would be a good idea to extend that motif into the house. I found a lamp for the entry room that had a similar leaf pattern. But I didn't want the whole place to look like a Roman palace—I wanted a house that told a story about who I was. The front could have a classical theme, but that theme would change gradually as you moved through the house, eventually ending in an ultramodern kitchen.

I found color schemes that would guide the transition from one room into another. I raised the entrance to the living room and lowered the floors and ceilings in the dining room. I bought shiny metal Wolf appliances for the kitchen.

But the deeper I got into the story, the more I began to obsess over the tiniest details, like whether the hang of the drapes guided the eye in the right direction or how the color of a handle correlated to the hinges on the door. I first realized that I had a serious problem on my hands after I spent 7 hours at a lighting store, just overwhelmed by the number of decisions in front of me.

I have a tendency to overthink things. The details can get so out-of-control that they just mess me up. So I try, whenever I can, to minimize my options.

I've simplified my wardrobe: the T-shirt and jeans when it's casual, the bow tie when the situation demands something more. I always choose the same seat on airplanes. When I go out to eat, I go to restaurants where there are only two or three choices. Don't even show me a big menu—I'll just ask the waiter or waitress to choose something for me. And when I find something I like, whether it's a bottle of wine or a baked potato done a certain way, I'll order it every time.

I don't want to think about that stuff. When it's time for dessert, bring me vanilla ice cream. There are too many damn choices out there.

Why bother with all of them?

A good vanilla is a great ice cream.

Foundation

POSTCARD FROM NEW YORK CITY

New York might be the most amazing place in the world. But it's also one of the saddest. Everybody comes here with lofty ambitions, but how many achieve them? The vast majority of them aren't even going to find the d in "dream." Of 100 people, 70 are going to get stuck (or worse), 20 or 25 will struggle on to something better, maybe 5 will actually get somewhere. One or two of them might become success stories. But let's be real: The majority of people who are doing something great in New York City already had money in the first place. It can be a truly disheartening town.

New York will always be here. New York doesn't change. You have to understand the sadness of the city to understand that it's all right to leave, to go create something for yourself. Then you can come back and be the Guy, instead of the guy trying to keep up with all the other guys.

With all the things that I was doing in New York City, it might sound like football was an afterthought. But when it was time to focus on football, I got focused on football.

I couldn't wait to get back on the field. That first season, while I watched from the sidelines, the Giants went on a late-season run that led all the way to the Super Bowl. I couldn't believe what I was missing.

I showed up at the training facilities to rehab my knee every morning at 6:00, no matter how hammered I was from the night before. The more time you take feeling bad about an injury, the less time you're going to have to actually get better. Two weeks of self-pity over what might have been are 2 weeks that could have been applied toward your recovery.

As soon as I could start practicing again, I developed a deep relationship with water in its frozen form. Ice before practice. Ice after practice. Ice, lift weights, then ice again.

The second season finally arrived. I played special teams, and when linebacker Jessie Armstead got banged up, I filled in for him on third downs, when the opposition was more likely to be passing. I got my first interception in a comeback victory against the Cowboys, a rare bright spot in a season where we went 7-9 and missed the playoffs.

The next season, the Giants decided to cut costs and part ways with Armstead, an All-Pro and the heir apparent to Hall of Famer Lawrence Taylor. I was expected to step into his shoes at weak side linebacker—or what football people call the "Will"—the position I'd played my sophomore year of college.

Teams run most of their offensive plays to the "strong" side—usually the side where the tight end lines up—simply because it's the side with the most players to block the other team. The Will lines up defensively on the weak side—the side with fewer players. His greatest assets are speed, as he often finds himself pursuing the play rather than hitting it head-on, and the ability to wrap up and tackle players from behind, a skill that I'd developed as a high school wrestler.

I didn't make anyone forget about Jessie Armstead—or LT, for that matter—but I played well enough to help the team ride a late-season run into the playoffs. We were feeling good about our chances until those chances died in a brutal one-point loss at San Francisco; Giants fans may remember a long snapper named Trey Junkin and two botched field goal attempts.

On a personal level, my fourth season was a success—I finished second on the team in tackles—but the Giants as a whole did a lot worse: a 4-12 record. Management decided it was time for a change, firing the head coach, Jim Fassel, and his staff. The situation was changing for me, as well: The end of the season also meant the end of the original contract I'd signed with the Giants as a rookie.

The team was willing to re-sign me, but they didn't exactly seem enthusiastic. There was going to be a new coach—Tom Coughlin—and new coaches like to fill their teams with their kind of players. I had no idea whether or not I was a Tom Coughlin type of player.

My feelings about the changing situation: Take a little bit of ego, mix in a lot of ignorance, and add a pinch of the grass has got to be greener on the other side.

I decided to sign with a new agent, Happy Walters. Happy's firm, Immortal Sports and Entertainment, was one of the first agencies to focus on the emerging opportunities for crossover between sports and entertainment. They were going to help me get involved in music, television, and movies—at some point, anyway. For the time being, they were going to focus on finding me a bigger deal than what the Giants were offering.

During all this change, my parents were planning a trip to Jordan, where they were friends with the United States ambassador. I jumped at the chance to join them.

The situation in Jordan was a little schizophrenic. Amman, the capital, was in the midst of violence and upheaval. We travelled from place to place in a convoy of armored cars. Go out to eat, get up to go to the bathroom, and a bodyguard was going to follow you there.

Outside Amman was a different story. We travelled to Wadi Musa—literally the Valley of Moses. The unbelievably stark and still landscape, backdrop to the Bible, was a perfect antidote to whatever present-day chaos was going on back home. The wadi itself—a dry, rocky valley that becomes a river during the rainy season—reminded me that the pathways we travel are always shifting, often governed by forces far bigger than us.

We hiked through a narrow gorge to Petra, a 2,600-year-old city built into the side of a mountain, considered one of the modern-day Seven Wonders of the World. Even if you've never been there yourself, you may have seen it through the eyes of Indiana Jones or, more recently, the Transformers. I was feeling some of that transformation myself, scrambling up and down the rocky hills, whooping and hollering at the wide-open sky, feeling like a teenager with the whole world in front of him. One more (re)affirmation in my life: There's no experience more restorative than travel.

Even though I called my girlfriend every day—my cell phone doesn't work in my kitchen, but I got crystal-clear coverage in Petra—I felt a little stir-crazy when we got back to Amman, where all the security concerns put a serious crimp in any kind of nighttime social life or exploration. Looking for some kind of outlet for my energy, I noticed an old sewing machine in the corner and asked if I could try it out.

There were some scraps of Jordanian silk lying about, the perfect size for what I had in mind. I took a bow tie out of my bag and carefully took it apart, figuring out the cut of the cloth and the stitching that held it together. Before too long, I'd created a couple of new bow ties of my own design. I named my new venture Five Star Ties.

I didn't know what was going to happen next in my life, but I felt invigorated by the opportunities that lay ahead.

The "D-Word"
(Philadelphia)

Football schedules change from year to year, but one aspect remains constant: You have to play each of the other teams in your division twice. They say familiarity breeds contempt, which is why there are some great rivalries among teams in the same division.

But familiarity also breeds familiarity.

The Washington Redskins, for example, needed to upgrade their defensive line as they entered the 2004 season. They wanted someone as talented as the Giants' Cornelius Griffin, a player they knew well, having faced him two times every year. So they signed Cornelius Griffin.

The Giants needed a strong side linebacker, someone like the Philadelphia Eagles' defensive MVP, Carlos Emmons. They signed Carlos Emmons.

That left the Eagles with a hole to fill at linebacker. They chose me.

I hadn't played strong side linebacker (or "Sam") since college. As a weak side linebacker, I relied on my speed and agility to catch up with the play. On the strong side—the side of the field with extra blockers—I'd have to use brawn. The Sam usually has to fight his way past the tight end or fullback to make a head-on play against the guy with the ball.

Emmons was 4 inches taller and at least 10 pounds heavier than me. Some of the Philadelphia newspapers worried that the size difference was going to be a problem. I'd already encountered the same issue at Michigan. At the end of the day, I believed, football players were football players. I felt confident that I could handle it.

I'd laid my foundation, signing a 4-year deal with the Eagles. Now it was time for the next stage of my master plan: to prove that a football player could be a thinking man.

I looked for every opportunity to do so, from interviews with the media to the message on my answering machine.

"It's not about words, it's about energy. The source found within, around, and through you. If you believe in it, then move with it. Be a part of it. Understand it. Think about this as you leave a message for Dhani Jones."

But I felt like the best opportunity to change the world's perceptions would come from television. Not just as a faceless football player on Sundays—I wanted the world to see me without a helmet.

The NFL Network was just getting off the ground and was looking for players who could help put a face on the league. I participated in one of their training courses while I was with the Giants. Even though we failed to make the postseason during my final season in New York, I was still on the field during the playoffs and Super Bowl with a microphone and camera, interviewing players like Tom Brady and Ray Lewis. The next season, the NFL Network started *Total Access,* a sort of roundtable discussion among football players, helmets off, talking about football. I was a regular guest.

A NOTE FROM JONATHAN FIERRO, PRODUCER OF TIMELESS AND DHANI TACKLES THE GLOBE

Timeless was a series we produced for ESPN, a documentary about good sports stories. Not "What happened in the game last night?" It was the kind of stuff you wouldn't hear every day. Lama Kunga, a Buddhist priest in San Francisco, loves golf because "mulligans are very forgiving." A high school football player in Detroit has no legs. He's a defensive lineman and they let him play. He's actually pretty good.

ESPN liked it. We did three 1-hour pilots with Ralph Wiley, a writer from the New York Times, *as our host. ESPN green-lit 30 episodes. A month or two later, Ralph had a heart attack and died.*

And so the owners of the company are like, "What are you going to do about a host?"

I was reading GQ *when I saw a pictorial with him.* Dhani Jones, *I thought.* That guy used to play for the Giants. *The article said he played the washboard. I remembered seeing him on NY1, the local TV channel. I thought maybe I should meet with this guy. As long as he had a presence, that's what we needed. If he happened to be able to remember his lines or add something, that would be a bonus.*

So we went down to Philadelphia and met with him. A lot of ballplayers, you get the feeling they are looking past you, or they're just like, "Is it over yet?" But Dhani? Great interview. He was engaging. He had a presence right away. I don't think he wore the bow tie to that first meeting—he had just come from practice, so he was in sweats—but I could just tell. You know, you meet someone and the way they shake your hand or the way they look you in the eye when they talk about stuff. He was genuinely excited.

We brought the owners down. They loved him. Then we pitched him to ESPN, and they were like, "Sure, you can use anyone." And that's how it all started with Dhani and me. We did two seasons of Timeless *and won two Emmys.*

———

The Eagles weren't exactly thrilled that I'd be filming *Timeless* during the season, but the producer, Jonathan Fierro, was willing to work with my schedule. We filmed on Tuesdays, my days off, and most of the time the New York–based crew travelled to Philadelphia to meet me. Fierro was great at finding interesting places to shoot my bits, like the abandoned Philadelphia Electric Company plant or the Eastern State Penitentiary, a supposedly haunted prison built in the 1820s.

But when it was time for football, I played football.

From an individual standpoint, my first season with the Eagles was decent, not great. As a team, however, we were spectacular. The Eagles had their best season in team history, winning 13 of the first 14 games. We were so far in front of the rest of our division that we rested our starters for the last two games of the regular season. The team had a reputation for making early exits from the playoffs, but we fought all the way to the Super Bowl, where we lost by three points to the Patriots.

———

The next season, by comparison, was an absolute nightmare. We lost a couple of key defensive players to free agency. Everybody on offense seemed to be injured, mired in some kind of contract dispute, or both. We started 3-1 before the wheels fell off the proverbial wagon—we finished the season 6-10.

Against this dysfunctional backdrop, my off-the-field interests and activities started to seem like an issue.

When you do a lot of different things in high school or college, most people pat you on the back and call you well-rounded. When you do the same thing in the NFL, you start to hear the D-word: "distracted."

Football has come a long way over the years, but there are aspects of the game that are still stuck in the 1950s. Most coaches don't want independent thinkers or players who might challenge their authority. Individuality is not exactly encouraged in a league where, as the expression goes, fans root for the laundry, not the human beings who are wearing it. You play football, you think football, and you eat football. What's on your mind when you wake up in the morning? Football. When you go to bed? Football. What do you watch on TV when you're not playing football? Football.

The fact that I was doing TV meant that I was valuing "off-the-field" more than "on-the-field."

Then there were the announcers who played my latest voicemail message—on national TV—during a game against Carolina.

"Change. The inevitable. A point in one's life where all that exists begins again. And the historical enigma presents itself. Don't be afraid . . . as you leave a message for Dhani Jones. For life is change, and change is life."

Maybe they weren't exactly ridiculing me, but they weren't exactly paying me a compliment, either.

Anyway, it felt like it didn't matter how hard I worked on football—people were still going to wonder how much better I'd be if the game wasn't just my primary focus, but my *only* focus.

I had the locker next to Mark Simoneau, the Eagles' middle linebacker. We called him "Simonowski," after Bill Romanowski, the former Pro Bowl linebacker for the Raiders known for his commitment to improving his body through supplements—some legal, some less so. Simoneau was always taking some sort of pill or another. I wanted to know more.

We started spending more time together. One day I went over to his house, where I found him getting soft tissue therapy—a massage technique used to alleviate muscle pain and tightness—from a guy named Tim Adams. I asked Tim if he'd be willing to do the same for me.

As Tim began working on me, I started asking him questions. He claimed he wasn't just a masseur, but a personal trainer who could do everything from strength and speed training to mental conditioning.

"That's impossible," I said. "You can't do all that."

"Give me a try," he replied.

As we kept talking, Tim slowly began to open up about his belief system. He talked about modalities, work capacity, and the importance of core stability. He made me think about how my body was pieced together, ideas that I hadn't really considered since my anatomy classes in college. He told me about the mentors he had studied with, trainers from Spain to Japan who were exploring the cutting edge of athletic performance.

Tim was communicating with me in a way that no one else was. "If you really want to make your mark in this league, you really have to take charge of who you are as an athlete," he said. "There are so many people who will try to control you. You have to have your own internal focus and balance, of a substantial strength, that can't be shaken. You need to plant your feet in the ground."

By the time the conversation was over, I'd made a decision: I wanted to train with Tim.

This might sound like a pretty easy decision to make.

It wasn't.

As I said earlier, the NFL doesn't encourage individuality. There is no shortage of people who will try to control you. Every team has an owner, an administrative staff, a head coach, dozens of assistant coaches, doctors, trainers, physical therapists, even priests, all of whom have their own ideas about what you need to do to be your best. Players are the teams' investments, and the teams want to protect those investments.

No one is going to stop you from hiring your own trainer or developing your own workouts, but they'll let you know, in no uncertain terms, that you're out there on your own. As far as the team is concerned, you're on an island.

If everything goes well, they may build a bridge, allowing you to come back over.

Or they might just say, "Fuck that bridge. You've got to stay over there by yourself. You made a decision. That's what you've got to rock with."

Dancing in the Streets

You might remember, earlier in the book, when I talked about the conference table in my head. One of the guys at the table is the Angry Guy. I do my best to tire him out, to keep him sleeping in the corner.

It's March, and I'm dancing at a club in South Beach. The cops are breaking up the party. Everybody's trying to get to the door. People are spilling into the street, where there are more cops telling everybody where to go. "Move here. Not over there. Over here."

I'm not done dancing yet.

The Angry Guy wakes up and says, "Man, why don't you just leave us the fuck alone?" And once he wakes up and engages in battle, it's not so easy to put him back in the corner.

So I keep dancing, despite several requests from the police to clear the area. I didn't really give them any choice but to slap the cuffs on me.

At least now I've got some cred with the convicts—"Yeah, I've been arrested"—before I make them laugh by telling them it was for dancing in the streets.

The Feel-Good Space

A NOTE FROM TIM ADAMS, PERSONAL TRAINER AND AUTHOR OF *MAKING THE BEST BETTER*

I was in the military for quite a while, and I had the opportunity to be exposed to some of the Air Force Special Forces. And they have this terminology to describe a part of their training.

Actually, two different terminologies, depending on whom you're talking to:

The commander uses "feel-good." As in, "You're going to get into this feel-good space." The feel-good space is what the grunts and the guys who are out in the field end up calling "suck it the fuck up."

It's a dark space. And I really like putting guys in that dark space, or that feel-good space, because that's when you grow—not only physiologically, but as a person, from a mental perspective.

It's not like I'm going to put you in that space every single day. But every week you're going to be in that space.

Everybody's space is different. I've got guys who can run forever, so that's not going to do it. But if you make them do repeat sprints, you're going to blow them up. Whereas if you get a guy who loves to sprint, but you make him do 3 minutes of continuous running, you'll blow him up. It's about finding out what it is, that one thing.

It's actually pretty easy to do, because guys, especially professional athletes, they really don't like to do things that they are not good at. You find out what that thing is that they're not good at, and you reinforce it.

I don't just want to improve your strength. I want to improve your weaknesses. But I don't want to improve your weaknesses at the expense of your strength: I want everything to improve. Getting guys into the feel-good space helps to improve the whole system.

Sucking It the F*** Up

POSTCARD FROM PHILADELPHIA

I loved Philadelphia, but the feeling wasn't always mutual; it's a city whose sports fans seem to cheer loudest when they're driving their heroes out of town—just ask Allen Iverson, Charles Barkley, Eric Lindros, or Donovan McNabb. Their greatest hero—the one who gets a statue on the steps of the Museum of Art—is Rocky.

A fictional character.

When it comes to sports, Philadelphia is a city with expectations. You don't have to be perfect, but at times it feels like you're being graded not on a sliding scale, but on a rising bar, one that you'll never quite be able to reach.

In New York I always felt like an individual. I'd meet all kinds of people from all walks of life. Being a football player just made me one more fragment in a crazy mosaic.

When I went out in Philadelphia, I was, first and foremost, an Eagle. Part of the collective. Almost everybody I met wanted to talk football. I often felt like I was valued not for what I could add to the conversation, but for my perceived value to the team. It was a hard feeling to shake. I'd get bombarded for an hour or two before politely excusing myself and heading home.

I found myself going out less, instead reserving myself to my own world. I had a small group of friends, people who didn't necessarily live and breathe football. I also kept one foot firmly planted in New York City. Friday night I might take a train or hire a car service to go to some event in Manhattan. I'd party until 2:00 in the morning, make my way back to Philly, and sneak in a couple hours of sleep before going to practice.

In retrospect, it's clear to me that the problem wasn't all Philadelphia. There were as many ways for me to branch out there as anyplace else I've ever lived. I'm sure I missed a few. Maybe my maturity level wasn't high enough for me to take advantage of the opportunities that were in front of me. I didn't have a strong enough sense of internal balance to maintain my own mind-set independent of the people around me.

In for a penny, in for a pound: Once I'd decided to start training with Tim, I was fully committed. I told the Eagles that I wouldn't be working out with the team that summer. Instead, I flew to Alicante, Spain, a beautiful city on the Mediterranean, to train with Dr. Guillermo Laich, one of Tim's mentors.

When I returned from Spain, I flew to Southern California, where I spent another month working out with Tim.

Tim became my chaperone. Everywhere I went, he went. "Yes, you can do that. No, you can't do that. Okay. Nope. Not today."

He completely changed my diet. For me, food meant McDonald's, Sprite, and Twinkies. He replaced them with chicken and green tea. We'd go certain places and he'd literally slap my hand if I reached for something bad.

We had fights. "Man, I just wish you'd leave me the fuck alone!" I'd scream. "Get out of here. Why are you even here?"

"Because you're paying me," he'd always answer.

Despite our battles, Tim became one of the most important people in my life. I was in pretty good shape before I met him, but he took my training to a whole new level, incorporating running, lifting, soft tissue work, chiropractic work, proper nutrition, and mental exercises. We used MAT (Muscle Activation Techniques), ART (Active Release Techniques), and acupuncture.

Tim had a knack for explaining his training techniques in a way that really resonated with me. He was also one of the most intuitive teachers I'd ever met, extremely skilled at reading my moods, knowing when to push me. And when to push me more.

California became more than a place to train—it became a state of mind. As the season approached, "Gotta get to California" became my mantra. Two days before the start of training camp, I put in a bid on a place in San Diego.

I didn't get to see my new house for a couple of months, when the Eagles had their first bye week, because once football was on, I was locked in. In addition to the physical training, Tim had helped me to build a new mental attitude: If you want to do something that you think is going to make you stronger—a better athlete, a better person, a better man—then you do it. People are going to say what they will. Don't worry about them. You go out there and you post the results. Let that be your mark.

I came into training camp with the Eagles and . . .

Ball.

I had the best training camp of my career. I was physically prepared, my mind-set correct.

Still, I felt uneasy. You know that weird vibe: You go in the office, you're looking around, and you're like, "Why is everybody staring at me?" But they're not looking at you, not directly. They're whispering. You can't understand what they're saying, but you know it's not good.

I hadn't helped myself by getting arrested in Miami or doing my off-season training apart from the team. But no matter how hard I worked, I wasn't getting any feedback from the coaches—no reassurances that I was doing something right, no criticism to let me know what I was doing wrong. I felt like I was trying to live up to my father's expectations, only I didn't know what those expectations were. So I just kind of tried hard, tried hard, tried harder. My frustration grew. *Why don't you just tell me what you want me to do?*

The Eagles used the draft to bring in a younger linebacker to compete with me, and they seemed to be giving him every chance to succeed. I didn't have any problem with that—there are very few players in the NFL whose jobs aren't up for grabs. Every year is a fight to get the position you want or to keep the one you have. It's part of what makes the game great.

I won when the competition went down with a season-ending injury. I felt like I'd earned the job, but I wasn't sure that my coaches felt the same way. I got the sense that, in the eyes of some, I'd won by default.

———

We rebounded from the previous year's nightmare. The team showed a lot of character: Despite losing our star quarterback, Donovan McNabb, to an injury midway through the season, we finished 10-6 and won the division. We lost in the second round of the playoffs, but the general consensus seemed to be that the Eagles had done all right, all things considered.

Only the whispering didn't subside—it got louder. I'd turned in another decent season, but "decent" didn't seem to be satisfying anyone in Philadelphia. The Eagles used the beginning of the free agent period to add Takeo Spikes, a Pro Bowl linebacker. The local newspapers seemed to be writing about me in the past tense. But I was still on the team when the draft rolled around. Maybe it wasn't as bad as I thought.

Twenty-four hours after the draft, I got the news: The Eagles were cutting me.

I'd made my own decisions.

I'd created my own island.

Now I had to rock with it.

You've Got to Suffer

When your body is a tool, and your day job involves using that tool to slam, again and again, into extremely large human beings who have been trained to treat their bodies with the same level of disregard—each time generating an impact with roughly the same force as a car accident—you had better be ready for pain to become a constant companion.

A big part of football is learning how to manage that pain. We use massage and acupuncture, saunas and ice baths, daily supplements of vitamins and herbs. We combine the latest science—ART, MAT, and TENS (transcutaneous electrical nerve stimulation)—with ancient practices like the 3,000-year-old Chinese art of applying hot cups to different parts of the body. We pay frequent visits to stem machines, vibration platforms, hyperbaric chambers, oxygen concentrators, and lasers that zap our cells into healing faster.

I get a shot of Toradol—an anti-inflammatory and painkiller that was invented for horses—before every game. There are some players in the NFL who don't dose themselves with something to dull the pain as part of their pregame ritual. They are all rookies. Nobody's playing "sober" by his third or fourth season.

But no matter what you do, you can't eliminate the pain, at least not before the season is over. Nor would you want to.

Pain is information.

Over time, I have learned the power of routines. I stick to a specific diet and a defined way of working out with a certain level (or levels) of intensity. The routines help me to feel a certain way, to operate at a steady baseline that keeps me sensitive to any disruption to the norm. Those disruptions usually manifest themselves as pain, telling me instantly that something is wrong with my body or my lifestyle.

The key to routine is consistency. You have to stick to the plan. You've got to lift even if you don't want to lift. You've got to lift heavy when it's time to lift heavy and lift light when it's time to lift light. You've got to run when you don't want to run, more when you want to do less, faster when you want to go slower.

In other words, you've got to *suffer*.

Many guys, when they get into the league, they don't want to suffer. They haven't yet learned one of football's most profound secrets: When you suffer more, you'll suffer less.

Life is the same way.

Look at a newborn baby: He opens his eyes, breathes oxygen for the first time, and starts to cry. Maybe for about 6 months straight. Adults couldn't imagine living without light and air, but for a baby fresh out of the womb, it's pure pain.

Everybody's looking at the baby, but nobody notices the old man in the corner. If you did, you might see him grinning quietly, despite suffering from pain that the baby would find completely unimaginable—chronic aches and arthritis, a deteriorating body and mind, the knowledge that the days ahead are numbered. So what? He's heard everything, seen everything, felt everything, and tried everything. He has suffered, which is what allows him to relax in the face of all that pain.

You have got to suffer.

I suffer all the time. Every year, somehow, some way. But I don't let the suffering get in the way of success—there is no success without suffering. The more you suffer, the more you succeed.

Survival Mode

My life was in transition before the Eagles cut me. I bought the house in San Diego. I also found out from my agent, Happy Walters, that his firm was going to be restructuring; I was going to be assigned to a different representative. My intuition told me that if they were changing, maybe I should be changing, too.

Only every time I tried to think about it, my intuition started to get cluttered. My mind was like a hive of buzzing bees. I felt like I did when I got caught up in decorating my townhouse in New Jersey, unable to make what should have been simple decisions.

I needed an unbiased opinion. My financial advisor at the time, Leslie Giordano, told me that she could help. We both created lists of potential new agents, then whittled them down until there were only a few names left. She vetted the survivors and gave me a name: Don Yee.

I was sitting in my car, about to go eat with some friends in the Northern Liberties area of Philadelphia, when Don returned my call. I have to confess that I wasn't prepared for what was going to happen next.

Don broke me down.

He broke me down in a way that nobody besides my father had ever broken me down before. I immediately got the sense that Don understood my personality, where I was coming from, and what I had been through. He talked about the personalities of my coaches, the team ownership, and the league itself. He spoke with honesty—brutal honesty, at times—about my decisions and the perception of me they had helped to create.

By the end of the conversation, I was crying.

I also had a new agent.

A NOTE FROM DON YEE, AGENT

In our industry, generally speaking, when a player comes to you after he's had a divorce from another agent, sometimes he's picked up some bad habits. The model a lot of athletes have in their minds is that "The agent works for me."

I am looking for a more collegial relationship with my clients, one where we're working together. So when I initially spoke with Dhani, I was also interviewing him.

My opinion at that time, and this was just from afar, was that he was a good player who, perhaps, had a lot of other interests outside of football that could be taking some of his energy away from his primary job. He was fairly exposed in the media. When he'd make a good play—football is an emotional game, obviously—I felt there was a lot of energy being spent on postplay celebration. So I didn't know what to expect from him.

When I spoke with him, the feeling I came away with was different from my first impression. I remember feeling that it was very refreshing to talk to a guy who seemed very open-minded about taking some advice and guidance. He didn't act like a know-it-all with me, even though he was a veteran player at the time. He appeared to be actually listening to what I was saying, and—I think this is the biggest thing—he allowed himself to participate in someone else's vision for who he could be.

Dhani is an intelligent guy, but when you get to any level of professional sports, the most difficult terrain that an athlete has to navigate is the terrain between his ears. I tried to communicate very directly with him, without using clichés. He was at a point in his career where people in the industry were thinking that his productivity was never going to really get back to the same level as it was when he was a younger player.

I described my vision for him as a productive player.

Number one, I didn't want him to overthink every single potential business angle that could arise. In fact, I didn't want him to think about the business of the game at all, but to trust me to think about that for him.

Number two, I wanted him to simply connect with what he liked about the game, not to think about how success could lead to X, Y, and Z, or monetary gain. I wanted him to focus on the camaraderie.

I often ask athletes, "Why are you even in this endeavor in the first place?" And if the answer is "I want to make money," that tells me something.

But if the answer is "Well, it's a lot of fun. I like playing and the feeling I get from playing. I like the guys in the locker room. And if I happen to do well and I make money, so be it. I'm just lucky to do something that I like," that's different. Like I said, I was interviewing Dhani at the same time he was interviewing me.

When I saw that Dhani was open and flexible and receptive to taking advice, there was a clear signaling to me that he really was maturing emotionally and intellectually. I sensed that he wanted to get more grounded and have a firmer plan. And when he sensed that I wanted to nurture and help him trust that grounded feeling, I knew we were going to have a good relationship.

Don's first advice to me? Change my voicemail. No more thought-provoking quotes. The coaches don't need to be reminded that you have a brain.

I changed the voicemail. I haven't changed it since.

"You've reached the voicemail of Dhani Jones. Please leave a message."

That wasn't enough to save my job with the Eagles. When I got released, Don assured me that it was only a matter of time before I got picked up by another team. But the first round of free agency had already come and gone. I began to question my future.

Was I changing gears?

Was I entering the next phase of my life?

I didn't know.

I sat down on the beach near my house in San Diego and stared at the ocean. My brain went into survival mode.

When I go into survival mode, it's nothing like the buzzing of the hive. I become extremely focused. Methodical chaos. It's like *The Matrix*—in my mind's eye, I see organizational charts connecting names, numbers, and possibilities. The scenarios branch, weave, and merge to form new scenarios. I start laying tracks, imagining where my life could be 5, 10, 20 years down each road.

It wasn't too late for medical school.

I had business interests outside of football. The bow tie company. An Asian spirits venture I'd started with a friend of mine from New York.

I had my art. I was still taking photographs, and some of them were actually pretty good.

There were invitations to do public speaking.

I'd even been talking to Jonathan Fierro, the producer from

Timeless, about hosting my own show, one that would combine my interest in sports with my love of travel.

All these ideas flowed through my mind. I'd follow each one, imagining how they might branch off or intersect in the future. Laying down soft tracks that, through action, could become hard tracks.

Then I got a call from the Saints.

I was ecstatic to have a second chance. Some friends helped me pack my bags. I was going to keep my place in California, but I was going to begin building a new foundation in New Orleans, where I could reinvent my career with the Saints.

Two days before training camp, the phone rang again. It was Jonathan Fierro. He'd been pitching a show, *Dhani Tackles the Globe,* and the Travel Channel was interested. But they wanted to see a "sizzle reel," a sort of abbreviated episode that conveyed a sense of what the show was about.

Could I fly to New York to shoot it?

The conventional wisdom, some might suggest, would be to say no. It was 2 days before camp, time to focus on football, on salvaging my career.

I was working out with Tim, so I asked him what he thought.

"Hell yeah, you should do it!" he replied.

Really?

"Sometimes a window opens," he continued. "Either you're going to jump through, allow it to close behind you, and see what's on the other side, or you're going to stand and watch the window close. But you're never going to see what could have happened on the other side."

Made sense to me.

The next thing I knew, I was in New York City, learning salsa dancing and handball for a show that might never happen.

Wishing, Not Wanting

T he peak summer temperature in Jackson, Mississippi, where the New Orleans Saints hold their training camp, is usually 91 degrees.

It was at least 10 degrees hotter than that. And I was in the South. I'm a north-of-the-Mason-Dixon-line kind of guy. Wasn't this where *Mississippi Burning* happened?

My body felt terrible. I felt like I was moving in slow motion. My mind started playing tricks on me.

The Saints already had their linebackers: Scott Shanle, Scott Fujita, and my old friend from Philadelphia, Mark Simoneau. They were "the Snow Patrol"—the only all-white linebacking corps in the NFL.

I was competing for Fujita's position. The coaches loved Fujita. The fans loved Fujita. No way I was going to beat out Fujita.

So I was there to be a backup. But they already had a backup in Brian Simmons. Why was I here? How could Don actually think this was a good idea? Maybe I hadn't chosen the right agent after all.

It was hot. Hot as hell. I played a couple of exhibition games and did all right, but "all right" wasn't going to make the squad.

It was miserable, but that's football. Sometimes football means triumph and exhilaration. Sometimes football means getting called into an office, after 3 painful weeks puking up your guts in training camp, so you can find out that you didn't make the team.

I got called into the office. Coach Sean Payton thanked me for my time, but they were going to have to let me go.

Peace out.

———

Back in California, Don kept reassuring me. This is how the process works.

Something's going to happen.

Somebody's going to go down.

Somebody's not going to be happy with something.

Wait a couple of games.

I was called in to visit other teams. A workout in DC with the Redskins. Another in Tennessee with the Titans. Off to Buffalo to see the Bills.

Buffalo? I didn't want to be in Buffalo. It's dead in Buffalo. Best thing about Buffalo is that it's close to Canada.

I smiled and shook a lot of hands. I ran sprints in front of guys with stopwatches. And all the time I'm thinking, *Don't pick me. Don't pick me. Don't. Pick. Me.*

Wishing for a job, but not wanting a job.

———

The season started without me. I was back on the beach in San Diego. *Here is the water,* I told myself. *This is where you want to live. You're good.*

Sure, there had been a wrench in my plans. But was it really a wrench? So football was over. That just meant the rest of my life was about to begin.

I lifted and ran. Read a few books. Took a lot of "me" time, thinking about everything that was going on and everything that wasn't. I was trying to get a sense of where I was so that I could start making plans for whatever came next.

Two games into the season, the phone rang. The Bengals wanted to meet with me in Cincinnati. "This might be a good fit," Don said. "I know Marvin. He likes you. He's seen you."

You never know where people are watching you. "Marvin" was the Bengals' head coach, Marvin Lewis. During camp with the Saints, we'd done an intersquad workout with his team, where Coach Lewis had seen me practice. He'd been a coach with the Redskins during my years with the Giants and had seen me play there. Everybody's got their board, the players they're interested in, and I was apparently on Marvin's.

There wasn't any car waiting for me when I arrived in Cincinnati, so I took a cab to the Bengals' facilities. Coach Lewis and the rest of the management team took me to a dark room with no windows.

"We'd like to sign you," they told me, "but we're a little concerned about your back."

My back?

It took me a minute to realize they were talking about the diskectomy I'd had in high school. Which hadn't been an issue *since* high school.

The Bengals wanted me to sign a waiver releasing them from any contractual obligations should my back turn out to be a problem. Don said no. They argued back and forth. All I wanted to do was get out of there.

Nothing had been resolved when I left for my hotel room. *This is it,* I told myself. *This is my last spot. I'm going to go do something else.* I called Don. "Put me on the next flight out of here." No flights to California until tomorrow. "Then book me for tomorrow."

Then Don called again. They'd resolved the waiver issue. The Bengals wanted to sign me to a 1-year deal.

A NOTE FROM MARVIN LEWIS,
HEAD COACH OF THE BENGALS

My first impressions of Dhani, when he came into the league, were fine. My second impressions? I wondered how important football was to him with all the other things he was doing at that time.

But then we had the opportunity to spend time with him here in Cincinnati, when he was with the Saints, and I was impressed with him. He likes to talk and ask questions, but they're good questions. I guess that's been his mode since he came into the NFL. When we brought him in to work out and had interest in signing him, that was something that he said to me: "Coaches get mad at me because I ask too many questions. How are you going to be with this?"

And I said, as long as the questions are good questions and they're pertinent to what we're doing, I'm fine with it. If you want to know, that's great. Knowledge is power.

We wanted to sign a veteran player, because we felt a veteran player would get up to speed much quicker and be able to be productive much quicker. But what Dhani did from the onset is he accepted his role no matter what it was. That was key. And we had him to the house the first Thanksgiving he was here, he and his mom. After meeting Dhani's mother, you know where Dhani came from. So things don't surprise you.

The next day, the owner, Paul Brown Jr., visited me at my hotel. This was my owner? The man was as cool as a fan. I signed the contract, and the next day I began practicing with the team.

I needed a place to stay. Remembering my mom's advice from New York City—nothing is guaranteed—I decided not to lock myself into a long-term lease. The hotel I was staying in was kind of nice. And it was close enough to the stadium that I could ride a bike to work.

A NOTE FROM JACKIE TAGGART-BOYD, SENIOR SALES MANAGER, THE WESTIN CINCINNATI

One of my friends from high school called me and said that she had been talking to Dhani. He was thinking about just

living in the hotel for the rest of the season. Could I take care
of that?

I met him in the lobby on his first day here. I expected one of
two things. When we have teams come in, either the guys are
completely suited down and look quite professional, with their
BlackBerries or whatever. Or they are completely blinged
out—you know, the big white T-shirt and a hat on backwards.
So I expected one extreme or the other.

I did not expect a hippie.

That was just the word that came into my mind when I
saw him. Hippie.

Later, Dhani called me and asked if I knew where to get a
bicycle. Nobody expects a professional athlete to have a bicy-
cle. An Escalade towing a Porsche towing a Benz, you know?
To me, a bicycle is just basically what kids ride. But he was
pretty detailed about what he needed to have in a bicycle.

After every encounter with Dhani, I'd go back and Google
him again. Who is this guy? I'm confused. He doesn't match.
You can't put him in a box.

He was just being Dhani.

I rode my bike to and from the stadium every day, keeping my head
down, focusing on my new job.

I worked with Paul Guenther, the assistant linebacker coach, to
get up to speed. I didn't know the playbook yet, but that didn't really
matter. I was there to add depth at linebacker, where the Bengals had
suffered a few injuries. An insurance policy. I was going to play special
teams, just like I did at the start of my career.

At the press conference to announce my signing, someone asked
me if I was a weak side guy or a strong side guy.

"I'm a job guy," I answered.

I suited up the very first weekend I was there, the Bengals' third game of the season, eager to show my value on special teams against the Seattle Seahawks.

By halftime, three linebackers had gone down with injuries. There were only two left on the roster, including me. I was playing strong side *and* weak side.

The next game, against the Patriots, I was calling out the defensive plays for the coaching staff. Normally the play-calling responsibilities belong to the middle linebacker—the "Mike"—usually the de facto captain of the defense. But you can't have a middle linebacker when there are only two on the field.

I didn't necessarily make all the plays, but I got better as the season went along. In 14 games—and just nine starts—I finished with more tackles than I did in any year I was with the Eagles. Statistically speaking, it was my best year since my last season with the Giants.

The Bengals seemed to be improving as well. After a rough start, the team went 5-3 over the final eight games.

I felt rejuvenated, like an asset instead of a liability. The Bengals wanted to re-sign me, possibly to a longer-term deal. I was grateful for the opportunity and excited for the future.

Which is why I had to keep my next move a secret from *everyone.*

PART TWO

Tackling the Globe

Disorganized Chaos
(England)

No one can know where I'm going.

Can't tell my coaches. Best case scenario is they'll think I'm distracted. Worst case, I come home with two broken legs. Either way, I'm putting my NFL career, which only 6 months ago seemed like it might be over, right back into harm's way.

Can't tell my agent. He'll probably try to talk me out of it. Remind me about that career he's trying to help me rebuild. About that new contract he's working to get done.

Can't tell my family or friends. Last thing I want to do is put my family into a position where they've got to keep a secret. Start telling people, somebody's going to wind up slipping.

Only Tim. Have to tell Tim.

Hell, I'm going to have to bring him with me.

———

As my first season with the Bengals neared its end, I got a call from Jonathan Fierro. The Travel Channel bought off on the sizzle reel for *Dhani Tackles the Globe*. Now they wanted to see a pilot episode.

"Leave me alone," I said, remembering all of Don's advice about concentrating on the game. "No one's going to let me do a TV show if I suck at football." Then I forgot all about it and focused on making plays on the field.

Maybe not *all* about it. Two days after the season ended, I was on a plane to London.

The idea behind *Dhani Tackles the Globe* was simple: I'd spend a week in a foreign country, learn a new sport, train, and compete against the locals. The show appealed to me on every level: athletic competition, international travel, and the chance to confront and possibly redefine two stereotypes that really bothered me; namely, that football players can't be cultured and that black people don't travel.

But I knew the idea would seem a lot less appealing to the Bengals, who were interested in signing me to a multiyear deal. The last thing they wanted to hear was that I was going to spend my off-season playing rugby.

The idea for rugby came from Pat Younge, then the general manager of the Travel Channel. Pat, who is black, was trying to bring some diversity to the network. How many black men have you seen hosting travel shows? There aren't a lot of black television hosts out there in any genre. Maybe we weren't making history, but we were at least trying to put a dent in it.

More importantly, Pat is from England. While the British might admit that it takes some toughness to play the game Americans have foolishly mislabeled as "football" (a term the Brits use to describe the game we oddly call "soccer"), it certainly isn't as tough a game as rugby. Helmets? Pads? What a bunch of divas!

When Pat suggested that we start with rugby, I felt like he was challenging my commitment to the show. Not only did he want to see if I could survive as a host, but he wanted to know if I was willing to bring some physicality to my role. *Let's see how ballsy Dhani is,* I could imagine him thinking. *Does he really want to do this show?* He may have also suspected that there was something in my makeup, my DNA, that prevents me from shying away from challenges.

It was on.

Still, sitting on that plane to London, I couldn't help but ask myself a single question.

What the fuck have I gotten myself into?

I kept reminding myself that I was doing what I wanted to do. Everything was going to work out for the best. This was what I was meant to be doing.

At least I hoped so.

Regardless of the outcome, I felt like I had to keep my activities secret from everyone. I was already fighting a reputation as a guy who gets distracted. From an outside perspective, I could see how it might look like I was now *extremely* distracted.

But I had to bring Tim. Once I was done showing those rugby players how easy their sport really was, I'd need someone to help me stay in football shape during my downtime. And if, for some reason, rugby turned out to be harder than football, I'd need Tim to help me keep my ego from destroying my body.

POSTCARD FROM ENGLAND

I thought it might be tough to get to know the English, given that I've never gone pheasant hunting on my "week's end." But they love to talk as much as I do, intense discussions over everything from sports to politics. And they love to drink— man, do they love to drink. In America, you might leave a liquor store carrying your purchases in a cardboard box. Here, they cart home their supplies using a dolly.

I remember my first day on *Timeless,* the show I did with Jonathan Fierro while I was with the Eagles. He asked me if I wanted to use a teleprompter to remember my lines.

"Hell no," I said. I was used to memorizing playbooks—how hard could it be to memorize and perform an introduction, a short bit in the middle, and a conclusion to a half-hour show?

Approximately 12 hours, as it turned out. Not exactly the best first day on the job.

By the end of the second season—long after I'd conceded to using a teleprompter—we were knocking out three shows in less than half that time.

When you're starting a new show, you generally don't know what the hell you are doing. We had a vague sense of what we thought Pat and the Travel Channel wanted—Is my sport tougher than yours?—but everything else was a blank slate.

Only thing to do with a blank slate is fill it.

Plan A: We spend a lot of time brainstorming ideas, debating plans, getting organized.

Plan B: We decide to say to hell with any organization; let's go balls to the wall and have the time of our lives doing it.

After no debate whatsoever, we agreed on Plan B. If the show gets picked up, it's going to be amazing. If it doesn't get picked up, then at least we had an amazing time.

We worked all day and partied like rock stars all night. Nobody went to bed until 3:00 or 4:00 in the morning. Call time was always at 6:00 a.m. Go hard or go home. I didn't have any time to think about what was happening. I figured it was part of my hazing, the Is-Dhani-tough-enough-to-handle-this?

So I just went with the flow. Somewhere in the middle of all this chaos, I managed to learn rugby.

RUGBY

According to local legend, rugby began in the 1820s at the Rugby School in Warwickshire. They'd already been playing football (the game we Americans insist on calling soccer) there for about 3 centuries before one of the students decided to pick up the ball and run with it. Definitely an asshole move. Not surprisingly, everybody else decided to chase him down and tackle him.

The "ball" was originally a pig bladder. About 50 years later, they switched to rubber inner tubes that had a tendency to flatten into more of an egglike shape. The players decided that they preferred the new ball, probably because they were sick of running around with a pig bladder in their hands. The modern rugby ball came into existence.

The field looks a lot like an old-school American football field with H-shaped goalposts. But it's about 30 feet longer, since the English, like pretty much everybody else in the world, use meters instead of yards. The basic rules are similar to football—no surprise, as football is based on rugby. Teams try to get the ball across the goal line—called a "try" instead of a touchdown—to earn five points. They can also score "drop goals," which are like field goals except that the kicker has to let the ball bounce off the ground before he kicks it.

Unlike football, there's no passing game; you can only toss the ball laterally or behind you. Blocking isn't allowed, either—you're only allowed to tackle the guy with the ball, who has to give it up when he hits the ground.

Which might make you think there isn't a lot of contact. You'd be wrong. There aren't any first downs in rugby—any issues over possession of the ball are settled by "rucks," "mauls," and "scrums." These are actually three very different activities, but they all look very similar to the untrained eye: violent, chaotic wrestling matches that sometimes involve every player on the field.

Each team has 15 players, who play two 40-minute halves—without time-outs or substitutions. You come out of the game, you're out of the game. The only exception is if you're bleeding a lot, in which case you can come out just long enough for someone to bandage your wounds. Nobody wears pads or protective facegear, aside from maybe taping the ears to the side of the head so they don't get ripped off. So, as you can probably guess, bleeding is a pretty big part of the game.

The Daily Telegraph
31 January 2008
DHANI JONES IS A BIG HIT AT BLACKHEATH
by Brendan Gallagher

Dhani Jones, the power-packed Cincinnati Bengals line-backer who famously got arrested two years ago because he would not stop dancing in a Miami street, is set to make his rugby debut for Blackheath against Launceston in the EDF Cup this week.

The engaging Jones is something of a television personality stateside and as part of a travel show he is putting together on England he wrote to Blackheath, the world's oldest open club who are celebrating their 150th anniversary season, requesting a game and permission to film a typical English club in action, on and off the field. Dangerous territory.

I was going to learn the game from a team called Blackheath. It didn't mean anything to me at the start, but it probably should have: When the Cincinnati Bengals were formed, in 1968, the Blackheath Football Club had already been in existence for 110 years. It's the team that Dr. Watson, Sherlock Holmes's sidekick, supposedly played for.

I hadn't heard of my guide, Austin Healey, either, which turned out to be another example of cultural ignorance on my part. "The Leicester Lip" is a celebrity in England. He's represented England in more than 50 international matches and also made the quarterfinals in *Strictly Come Dancing,* the show we "borrowed" and changed into *Dancing with the Stars.*

Austin and I sat down at a pub—virtually every discussion in England takes place over drinks, and there are a lot of discussions—and began arguing over the question we wanted the pilot to answer: Which is the tougher game, rugby or football?

"You guys wear helmets and pads," he said.

"So did the gladiators," I replied. "It makes the game more violent, not less. We hit each other harder."

"Yeah? You ever been injured?"

"Missed my whole rookie season with a torn ACL."

"Ha! I tore my ACL and PCL, snapped all the cartilage in my knee, and still suited up for a cap against Munster."

Maybe the conversation didn't go exactly like that—I was drunk halfway through—but you get the idea. The next day, I put on a pair of the itty-bitty shorts they call a uniform and showed up to practice with Blackheath on a day they called "Bloody Tuesday."

BLACKHEATH'S BLOODY TUESDAY DRILL

One guy holds a rugby ball, facing two guys in front of him. Those two guys get knocked over with a giant bag. They quickly pick themselves back up and tackle the guy with the ball as hard as they can. One of the tacklers goes to the back of the line, the ballcarrier becomes one of the tacklers, and the entire process gets repeated again.

And again.

And again.

A NOTE FROM TIM ADAMS, TRAINER

Dhani is a football player, so his priority is being ready to play come training camp. That was always in the back of my head: The reason why I was there was to ensure that he was safe in his environment and that he was doing what he needed to do in order to get prepared to play football.

And the very first drill I see, these guys are going 100 percent, no pads, just killing each other. And I'm going, Oh my gosh, what the hell did we just get ourselves into?

I don't even know what they call it, to be honest. Almost like an Oklahoma drill, where you put a guy in the middle and everybody on the outside is just going to go in and beat the shit out of him. Not just one guy on one guy; it was like two-on-one, three-on-one scenarios.

On the very first play of the drill, Dhani got knocked back. I think that kind of took him by surprise. I could see something change in his eyes. He was telling himself, All right, it's time to stop playing games and start getting serious.

I was in this dichotomy, being pulled in two directions. Do I pull him out of this because it's a dangerous drill? Or do I let him sit in it and experience this pain?

And I thought: Wow. This is actually great for him.

Every single activity that Dhani ended up doing for the show, I guarantee he got, at some point in time, into an uncomfortable space: the feel-good space. And I like that. My very first moment in England was my "aha" moment: This is going to be really good.

My body has never produced more lactic acid than it did on the rugby pitch.

In football, playing defense, the goal is always "three-and-out"—hold them for three plays and get the hell off the field. If you suck, you might be on the field for 12 plays. It probably averages out to something like seven plays per series.

I've had games, playing defense and special teams, where I've been on the field for more than 70 plays. That's uncommon. Exploding from a still position, 70 times over the course of maybe 3 hours, requires a shit-ton of stamina.

But in rugby, you *never* come off the field, except for a short break between the two 40-minute halves. By the end of the first practice, I was tired to my bones.

Another difference between football and rugby: the injuries. Not the number or severity of the injuries, but the way they get handled.

Football players shrug off injuries. Rugby players get downright festive about them.

"Oi, look at this, mate! I broke my fucking finger!"

"Fuck off, mate!"

"No, you fuck off!"

And the fights.

Despite all the physical contact, football players don't fight a lot. Too expensive—the league will fine you $20,000. But in rugby, fights are part of the sport itself. I mean, what is a scrum except an organized fight?

Did I mention that half of the guys on Blackheath are bankers?

Bankers. *Bankers!* This is what they do for recreation. They're out there beating the stuffing out of one another, a real-life Fight Club, for fun. Who the hell breaks their nose and calls it recreation?

Gritty people, the English.

The most remarkable feat of endurance might take place after the games. The stadium where Blackheath plays has 14 pubs inside. It's team tradition to crawl through them all after every game. I'm not talking about taking a shot or a sip of beer—there were guys chugging back entire bottles of wine. At. Each. Stop.

End of the crawl, some of the guys will stop at the liquor store before boarding the train home. Forget about a bottle wrapped in a paper bag—these guys are walking out of the store pushing dollies.

Bloody hell.

What's more dangerous than playing rugby?

Filming a TV show.

Since this was for the Travel Channel, there had to be an element of travel involved. One of the trips took us to the countryside for an afternoon of fox hunting.

We weren't really hunting. No guns. No foxes. None of that is really legal anymore. People just put on the clothes and go through the motions. Not the same thrill, but enough of one, I guess.

I climbed into a pair of riding pants and onto a horse. I was, of course, hung over as hell.

It's not easy to pee off the side of a horse.

I'd been on a horse before. But doing a 6-mile trot-and-canter when your body is already a giant knot of aches and pains was not the most pleasant experience in the world. *This is what you do,* I told myself, *if you want to be on TV.*

Near the end of the 6 miles, the riders at the head of the group blasted down a hill and jumped their horses over a fence. I was expected to follow, and, like a good television host, I did.

Having an offensive lineman fall on you can hurt. Some of those dudes weigh close to 400 pounds.

Horses weigh between 1,000 and 2,000 pounds. Having one hurdle you, right after he's thrown you off his back onto the ground, is some scary-ass shit.

But somehow he missed the opportunity to trample me to death. I brushed myself off and tried it again, this time going uphill at a more reasonable pace.

The things I do to be on television.

My actual game experience was over quickly.

Blackheath is a serious club. They weren't about to let a rank amateur spoil a chance at victory. The coach let me play the last 10 minutes of the game.

No one threw me the ball, but I did manage to make a couple of tackles, including one good enough to highlight on the show.

We'd done our time with rugby without destroying my football career. Mission accomplished, or at least in part—now we had to see if people would actually like the show.

GASSERS

They say a journey of a thousand miles begins with a single step. You can't run a marathon without first jogging a hundred feet.

That being said, the best way to prepare yourself to run a marathon isn't necessarily running a marathon.

Rugby players never leave the field, they play offense and defense, so endurance is clearly a priority. You have to get your wind right.

The coaches helped us to build that endurance using "gassers." We ran two laps around the pitch, rested for 30 seconds, then did it again until we'd repeated the process five times. After another 30-second break, we ran five single laps, then another five half laps.

This kind of "interval training" may not be just a good way to build endurance, but the *best* way. Several scientific studies have suggested that putting your body through these kinds of paces is a more effective way of building overall endurance than simply running long distances.

Let's say you're getting up after a long hibernation on the couch and you plan to run a 5-K. You could lace up your shoes, run as far as your current level of endurance will take you, pass out, and try it again the next day. And, over time, you'd get closer to your goal.

Or you could start with a leisurely 400-yard jog, just to relax and open your muscles. Then five 200-yard runs, separated by 30-second breaks, followed by five 100-yard and five 50-yard runs. Not only is it less psychologically intimidating to break a big run into smaller parts, but you'll make faster gains in your overall aerobic capacity.

Move Slowly Down the Hill

I once dated a girl from Scotland who took me to meet her grandmother for dinner. A pleasant evening—until the grandmother started dropping comments about *negroes* and *coloreds* into the conversation.

"Negroes?" I asked her. "Coloreds?"

"Well," she replied, "that's what you call them, isn't it?"

It dawned on me that she wasn't being racist, or even ignorant. That's what she knew. There may not have been any other words in her vocabulary to describe a black man.

The experience reminded me about the importance of going into each foreign culture with a clean slate. When I get to a new place, I try not to present myself in a way that forces people to react to me. It's on me to react to the people who live there, letting their ways and traditions take the lead.

I've definitely tried to do it the other way, arriving in a new country with an attitude that says, "I'm just going to change it up." The cities that really mess me up are the ones where I see a lot of beautiful women. I want to talk to everybody. So I do.

"Damn! Oh my gosh! Oh my goodness!" And then, "Hey, uh, hey, uh, where are you going? I . . ." They walk away. Run away. My ego gets smashed. (Or at least bruised.)

It's like that old joke about the two bulls at the top of the hill, father and son, who spot a herd of cows in the valley below. The son says, "Let's run down there and fuck two of those cows!"

And the father says, "We could do that, Son. But why don't we walk down slowly and fuck them all?"

I try to have a plan when I get to a new country. I don't want to sprint in and scare everybody off, leaving them to wonder, *What's his deal?* or *I just don't understand him.* I want to move slowly, taking the time to understand the people and their customs.

The plan isn't exactly a *plan,* but a mind-set. I'm going to spend my first day in any new country moving slowly, quietly, letting other people talk to me. I'm going to pay attention to the minor details: the inflections when they speak, the clothing they wear, the way they present themselves to you.

Do you greet one another with handshakes, kisses, or no contact at all? When you talk, do you stand close to the other person or far away? What do you talk about? Do men talk to women? Do women talk to women? How do you interact with kids? Do you even talk at all, or do you rely on a lot of nonverbal communication?

Who sits down first at the table, the men or the women? Who touches their food first? Do you use the fork in the left hand and the knife in the right, or the other way around? Do you use your hands? What kind of food do you like to eat? Is the food served all at one time or in smaller courses?

Do you walk with your hands at your sides, or do you place them behind your back? Where do you cross the road? Do you walk or run? Are the drivers fast or slow? Do they beep their horns?

What do you wear, and when? How often do you bathe? Wash your clothes? Do people smell good or do they stink, and do you care?

I'll spend my first day processing all this information, or as much as I possibly can. I'll use the details to create a laundry list in my mind, building a blueprint before I try to create an imprint.

On the second day, I'll take a deep breath and try to use my newfound understanding to engage people, slowly making my way into the culture. And I've found, more often than not, that people will receive me in a completely different way.

Organizing Chaos
(Ireland)

When we were finished in England, I needed a vacation. I settled on Dubai.

While I was there, I got a call from the TV producers. They wanted me to film some more footage, making the pilot a little less "Which sport is tougher?" and a little more sophisticated.

We returned to London and basically visited a few clubs, where instead of representing myself as a tough jock, I got to be suave and debonair, drinking champagne and kissing girls' hands.

Fine by me. I always wanted to be the first black James Bond.

I went from England to St. Barts, where I took my entire family to celebrate my 30th birthday. When I finally settled back into the United States, I got another birthday present.

I had played for the Bengals on a 1-year contract for the league's minimum salary. Come February 29, I was going to be a free agent without a team. But on March 1, the Bengals re-signed me to a 3-year deal worth a good bit more than the minimum.

A few weeks later I got a call from Jonathan Fierro. The Travel Channel wanted me to attend the "upfronts," the big meeting where the TV networks introduce potential new shows to advertisers and the media. That meant two things: (1) The show was almost definitely going to happen; and (2) people were going to start finding out about it.

One of those people was my agent, Don Yee.

"Why in the world didn't you tell me about this?" he asked.

The conversation turned into a real heart-to-heart, one that deepened our relationship. Don told me that he respected my judgment, that I was a grown man, and that he wasn't going to try to stop me from doing what I wanted to do. He just needed to know about it. "You've got to let me in on those secrets, the things that you've got going on. You don't have to tell your parents, but you better tell me!"

A NOTE FROM DON YEE, AGENT

When I found out that Dhani had been thrown from a horse while filming a TV show in England, well, I suspect there was a plan to avoid telling me. It appeared that I was the last guy to know. Moving forward, I tried to take a see-no-evil approach to his activities on the show. There's only so much that I can control.

I don't make decisions for any of my clients. I tell them that at the outset. I say my role is to just isolate the issues, analyze them, and if you want a recommendation, we will make it. But I really want them to be responsible for their own decisions. I would not have tried to talk him out of doing the show. I would've just simply pointed out the pluses and minuses, and let him make his own decision.

Let me give you a statistic: When Dhani went to the Bengals, the first contract was a minimum contract. And ultimately, the Bengals gave him an extension, a fairly lucrative extension, okay? Statistically speaking, when a veteran player accepts a minimum salary contract, the odds of that player ever seeing another contract in excess of the minimum are probably less than 10 percent. I don't think even he understands how well he has done.

The next phone call came from the Bengals' coach, Marvin Lewis. We'd only spent 1 year together and I had no idea what kind of beating I was in for, so I didn't pick it up the first time. The second time. The third time.

I finally picked it up the fourth time he called.

"So, how was it?" he asked. Then: "Because I want to live vicariously through you."

I started laughing, realizing that we were going to have a cool relationship.

A NOTE FROM MARVIN LEWIS, HEAD COACH OF THE BENGALS

I'm not one to worry much about what these guys do. They're the ones who are risking their careers. It's their career that they're having an opportunity to blow up if they're hurt in a nonfootball way.

Assume for a moment that you are a football player who is not spending the off-season scrumming with violent English bankers and falling off horses. What happens is the season ends—in December if you suck, February if you're great—and you take a much-needed vacation.

There are voluntary workouts with the team in March, but you're not actually required to report back to the field until the Organized Team Activities, or OTAs, for a few days in May. After a brief mini-camp for 3 days in June, you're off until the end of July, when official training camp begins.

For most players, the off-season is a chance for their bodies, minds, and souls to recover from the rigors of the season. For me in

2008, it became a jigsaw puzzle: How do I do all the things I have to do with the team while filming an international TV show?

The Travel Channel signed off on six episodes. The first, England, was already in the can. We would have to film the second, Ireland, in between OTAs and minicamp, then squeeze in four more shows in the month before training camp.

We had treated England like a crazy college road trip. Drinking all night, then waking up at 6:00 a.m. for workouts—both rugby and the extra stuff Tim had me do to maintain my football shape. Taking catnaps in the van as we drove from location to location, filming bits for the show.

There was no way in the world I could sustain that pace while keeping up my health, my energy levels, my athleticism, and everything else that went into keeping my day job. In Ireland we would have to figure out how to somehow organize the chaos while learning to play a game that was essentially just an excuse for grown men to beat on one another with wooden sticks.

POSTCARD FROM IRELAND

People complain that the food in Ireland isn't very fancy. Truth is, it's not. I don't want to compare it to an Old Country Buffet, but it's your basic hearty meal. Potatoes. Steak and potatoes. Corned beef and potatoes. Cabbage and potatoes. All of which is fine in my book.

Of course they love their whiskey and they love their Guinness. But it's not like they drink Guinness for breakfast—most days they wait until at least 11:00. I haven't seen any leprechauns or heard much talk of four-leaf clovers, but mention the North-South conflict and you'd better be ready to have an intense conversation for the next 45 minutes, one which could result in bloodshed.

And in terms of the sport of hurling, my biggest question is "What are they doing this for?" I mean, they basically just beat each other with sticks. There isn't any actual "hurling," whether you're talking about throwing a ball (which no one does because the game's played with sticks) or puking up your guts (which no one does because they're too prideful). It's like a double entendre where both things are misnamed.

HURLING

Imagine some mad scientist mixing lacrosse, baseball, and field hockey, then turning a dial to make it go much, much faster. Or a really violent form of golf, where players compete for a single ball while whacking one another with their clubs. Long before hurling became Ireland's second-most-popular sport (second only to soccer), it was actually a form of martial arts as old as storytelling itself, supposedly used by gods and wizards as they battled for the Irish countryside.

The sport, as it were, has been played for at least 2,000 years. During the 700s, rival villages used hurling to settle territorial disputes, engaging in massive free-for-alls that might involve hundreds of people. The earliest Irish laws spelled out procedures for compensating the families of the players who got killed during these "matches," which sometimes went on for days.

Hurling was so violent that it was outlawed during the 16th century. The ban only lasted for a couple of hundred years—by the 18th century, the "Golden Age of Hurling," landowners were competing against one another in order to entertain the serfs who worked for them. Nothing funnier than seeing your boss getting whacked with a wooden stick.

In simple terms, each team tries to get a small ball, called a *slio-tar,* into the opponent's goal using a wooden stick, the *hurley.* Ancient laws made it illegal for anyone, including kings, to take another man's hurley (although kings were allowed the unique privilege of lining their hurleys with metal). Today, they're still the Irish equivalent of baseball gloves, fathers proudly giving hurleys to their sons sometime around their second birthday, allowing them to knock the old sliotar around after work and on weekends.

Hurlers are allowed to catch, slap, or kick the sliotar, but if you want to run with it, you have to learn to bounce or balance it on the end of your hurley. Long passes and shots on goal are accomplished by dropping the ball and hitting it, like a baseball coach using a fungo bat, resulting in line drives that travel 100 miles per hour. As if the sport weren't chaotic or difficult enough, all these activities have to be managed while the opposing players slap at you with their sticks or try to knock you over with their shoulders.

I wanted to wear pads, gloves, and a helmet, especially after I heard one guy brag about losing his eyesight for 3 weeks following a blow to the head. My teammates laughed at my suggestion like I'd told the funniest joke in the world. It didn't seem as funny when I got slapped in the hand, which, despite my initial fear, did not shatter every one of my fingers.

(Oh, and by the way: Two years later, gloves and shin guards became an accepted part of the game. Helmets became mandatory.)

I was exhausted after my first practice—I was in shape, just not hurling shape. I looked around for the Gatorade, but was offered Guinness instead.

When in Dublin . . .

The second day—immediately following the football workout that Tim pushed me through—my hurling coach ran the team and me through an intense 45 minutes of drills: running up and down the field, moving laterally from sideline to sideline, slapping at the ball with our hands and our sticks, then trying to bounce it up and down on the end of the stick as we sprinted some more.

Then came the *actual* scrimmage, where we got to run up and down some more while grizzled old guys watched from the sidelines, murmuring about how much I sucked at this game.

Why was I doing this again?

We also had a travel show to film. After practice, we'd hop in a van and drive to a horse race. Or to shear a sheep—after I'd chased it down, like Rocky Balboa and the chicken.

One segment put me in front of a group of Irish kids who were learning American football. I got to channel my inner hard-ass coach, screaming at them as they did pushups and crunches. But every time I looked at the kids' faces, they were smiling, happy as hell to be exhausted and in pain, practicing a sport that almost no one in Ireland gave a damn about.

I thought about how the Irish talked about hurling, a game played almost exclusively on an amateur basis, with such passion and commitment. So what if they got tired or hurt? The game reminded them of who they were and what was important to them.

I thought some more about the conversations I'd had with Don about reconnecting with my love for football.

It doesn't make sense on any practical level, but there's something inside us that causes us to love the games we play—even when they are utterly kicking our ass.

KEEP THE SLIOTAR ON THE HURLEY

I've always considered myself blessed with good hand-eye coordination. The first time I ever played T-ball, I hit three home runs. I played a mean game of tennis and, growing up in Maryland, knew my way around a lacrosse stick.

That said, when it came to hurling, it took me something like 80 tries to hit the damn ball with the stick once the cameras started rolling.

It got a little easier with each drill, and I'm better for it. Even defensive football players need good hand- and foot-eye coordination to intercept passes and recover fumbles.

Assuming you don't have a hurley and a sliotar to call your own, you can approximate what we did by bouncing a tennis ball on a racquet while doing wind sprints and running figure eights. And when that gets too easy, start bouncing the ball on the *edge* of the racquet's frame instead of the strings.

You won't get the total hurling experience—you'd have to invite a bunch of friends to knock you around at the same time to do that—but you will get the benefits of a truly unique way of improving your coordination.

Washing My Clothes
in the Sink

T ravel is not just a gimmick I came up with for a television show. I love to travel. I'm always travelling. A friend of mine wrote a song called "Mr. Anywhere." Said it was about me.

I had a 2-week stretch last summer that took me from Cincinnati to New York City—for just 1 night—then on to Seoul, Korea, to visit my friend Bill. I went straight from Seoul to Beirut, Lebanon, where a friend from college met me for a few nights of partying. When the party slowed down, I kicked it back into gear in Dubai. Then it was Dubai to Los Angeles for the ESPYs, back to New York City for a weekend on a friend's yacht in the Hamptons, and a brief stop in Las Vegas for an awards ceremony before finally returning to Cincinnati to start training camp.

When you do that much travelling in such a short period of time, you've got to pack light. I carry one bag that's small enough to fit in the overhead compartment. We're talking three or four T-shirts and a couple of pairs of pants—this is where my "uniform" serves me well.

Right now you may be doing the math: four T-shirts, 14 days . . . no great mystery here—I wash them in the sink. I've become a master at turning hotel rooms into my personal Laundromat, hanging clothes in the shower, stringing them off balconies. I've lost stuff in the street, but it beats the hell out of carrying some huge steamer trunk around or spending all my money on hotel dry cleaning.

One of my favorite things about travel is that it pushes you out of your comfort zone. It reminds me that I know how to deal with all kinds of situations when I have to. I don't always like to deal with them, but it feels good to know that I can.

Getting into the Ring
(Thailand)

The 2008 Bengals began training camp on July 28. For the veterans, camp feels a lot like going back to school after summer vacation. You're happy to see the faces. Everyone's telling jokes, keeping spirits high for the two-a-day practices that are about to begin. And, of course, there's that familiar question: "What did you do over the summer?"

My summer vacation looked like this.

June 14 . . . . OTAs end; get on a plane that night to . . .

June 15–26 . . . . Thailand

June 26–July 5 . . . . Singapore

July 5–15 . . . . Switzerland

July 15–22 . . . . Spain

Four shows, 40 days, in four different parts of the world, then 2 days off until training camp. I knew I had to be serious with my preparation for the football season. Stay in shape. Stay focused.

And most of all, don't get hurt.

The trick was going to be doing all these things while somebody was trying his hardest to knock me unconscious.

MUAY THAI BOXING

It's human nature: The longer a civilization has been around, the more time they've spent trying to figure out how to kick one another's asses.

Thailand is located, more or less, between India and China, two of the most ancient cultures on earth. Muay Thai, Thailand's national sport, takes the best from more than 2,000 years of Chinese and Indian martial arts and synthesizes it into a unique fighting style often called the "Art of Eight Limbs." Its practitioners use two fists, two knees, two elbows, and two feet, making it extremely difficult for their opponents to defend themselves; pain can come from any direction.

What was originally used to fight wars is, today, the country's most popular form of entertainment. The matches take place in a boxing ring. Traditional drummers provide a soundtrack, beating slowly during the first round, gradually building in intensity to the frenzied third and final round. Thousands of people crowd into arenas to cheer for (and wager on) their favorite fighters, some of whom compete a couple of times a month. Not unlike the NFL, the average Muay Thai career does not last very long.

POSTCARD FROM THAILAND

You remember that old song from the 1980s? "One night in Bangkok makes a hard man humble/Not much between despair and ecstasy . . ." Well, it's all still true today. Brutal heat and ridiculous humidity. Everything is for sale, and everyone is fuckable: men, women, and the "lady boys" who are basically considered a third gender. Walk 15 feet off the street and you can see more traditionally defined "ladies" doing the nasty with donkeys or popping Ping-Pong balls out of their privates. You can see any show you want. You can make it up and take it anywhere you like. (Not that I did, of course—I'm all business on the road.)

The people eat whatever they can, including bugs. Especially bugs: beetles and bumblebees, caterpillars and cockroaches, and all manner of insect larvae. Turns out ants are the world's purest source of ATP, the molecule that the human body uses to store and transfer energy. You can see why the Thai have so much energy: they love eating ants.

They are also the most kind and generous people I have ever encountered. Everybody is friendly. They revere the elderly and their ancestors.

The country provides plenty of contradictions for my Western mind, but to the Thai it's just life, as normal as breathing.

The 21-hour flight to Bangkok gave me a lot of time for contemplation and reflection. I had no idea what was in store for me, but I was excited to find out—and committed to succeeding.

Still, I was going to Thailand to have a fight. I started thinking about falling off a horse in England, about nearly breaking my fingers in Ireland. I get hurt doing this, and my career—the one that pays me more per game than I could make in an entire season of doing this TV show—is over.

In my mind, I was going to have to treat this next adventure like I was Oscar de la Hoya, Roy Jones Jr., or Manny Pacquiao, sequestering myself from distractions, focusing on the fight, not really worrying about anything else. Work hard in the gym. Do what I have to do, both for football and for the show. Spend my nights getting plenty of sleep in my hotel room.

A NOTE FROM TIM ADAMS, TRAINER

I'll be honest with you. Fighting—the combative sports—was always at the top of my fears. Muay Thai is an extremely aggressive, extremely traumatic sport.

We walked into this training facility that we were using. And this young kid, he looks like he's maybe a buck-forty soaking wet, is doing a kicking drill. Another guy is holding a bag on his forearms, and this young kid is kicking it.

It's like a machine gun: Bam! Bam! Bam bam! Bam bam bam bam! *Not just fast, but there is a tremendous amount of force going into the bag.*

And I thought, This little kid is powerful. We're in deep, deep trouble here. If that lands on Dhani's ribs, he will break a rib. It's not a matter of if, it's a matter of when that's going to happen. *So I'm a little freaked out, this being my first day in Thailand. What the heck have we gotten ourselves into?*

Later, I find out the kid was the national champion. Not to take anything away from Dhani, but it was probably a good thing he didn't fight the national champion.

There's a world of difference between a football "fight"—which, to be honest, is generally a couple of guys wearing helmets, pushing and shoving just long enough for everyone else to break it up—and an organized match with a professional fighter. Fight on a football field, there are 50 guys who have your back. Step into the ring, and it's just you against an opponent who is hell-bent on causing you physical harm.

I like to say that nothing prepares you for football except football.

Well, it's also true that nothing prepares you to get hit in the face other than getting hit in the face.

I hadn't been in a fistfight since fifth grade, when some kid punched me in the side of the face. I remembered that it hurt then. But I figured that the years in between had toughened me up. And besides, my training partner, Pit, was wearing gloves, so it should hurt a lot less now.

Let's just say I was *green*. I figured wrong: Getting punched in the face still felt like getting punched in the face.

Real Muay Thai fighters like Pit don't wear protective pads. When I asked about headgear, Pit just laughed at me. So I went without—during training. But I didn't care how much people laughed at me: I wasn't going to get into the ring for my final match without headgear. Muhammad Ali once boasted, "My face is so pretty, you don't see a scar, which proves I'm king of the ring by far." I knew enough to know I was no Ali in the Muay Thai ring.

Here's another thing that you're unprepared for until you try it: eating bugs.

Fighting was only half of the episode—the rest of the show was about me exploring Thailand. So I visited Lumpinee Stadium, the Madison Square Garden of Muay Thai, to take in a fight. Got a reading from a fortune-teller; numerologically speaking, I was told the fight was likely to be successful, but I was in for a year of being unlucky at love. Visited the ruins of Ayutthaya, the ancient Thai capital that the rival Burmese laid waste to around the time America was revolting against the British. Experienced Chatuchak, otherwise known as "JJ Market"—imagine 42nd Street in its seedier days, only on crack—followed by Bangkok's infamous red light district, where you're never sure if the attractive woman tugging on your arm is actually a woman. I even played soccer with a baby elephant—if you ever try it, watch your toes, especially if you're wearing sandals.

In other words, we were doing the kind of stuff that I love to do when I'm travelling—interesting, fun, horizon broadening. Eating insects, however, was just *challenging.*

Like I've said, I'm a Twinkie and Sprite guy. But I'm always up for something new, so when Pit wanted to take me to lunch at a local street stall, I jumped at the chance. Turned out the only thing jumping was my lunch.

All right, so they weren't exactly jumping. All the crickets, bumblebees, grasshoppers, and their kin had been deep-fried in oil and seasoned with spices. The problem I had wasn't with the flavor, but the texture.

Or *textures.* The bugs were crunchy on the outside, but when I bit down, I felt the insides of my cheeks get sprayed by a thick goo. My throat closed up. My stomach rose up.

Why did I want to be on TV again?

PIT'S CORE-STRENGTH DRILL

The most important part of an all-wheel-drive car is the drivetrain— the transmission, the differentials, the driveshaft, all those hidden parts that make sure the power being generated in the front of the vehicle is balanced with the power in the rear.

Your core strength—upper abs, lower abs, midback, lower back, and obliques—is your drivetrain. These are the muscles that help you transfer energy between your upper and lower body. You might be able to bench-press 500 pounds or squat-thrust a small car, but if your core muscles aren't developed, you won't be able to transfer that power from one part of your body to another with maximum efficiency. You're going to overwork certain muscles, fatiguing them faster, burning out long before you should.

Combative sports that involve punching and kicking force you to twist your midsection, providing a great core-strength workout. But when you're fighting, it's not enough for your core to be strong; it also has to be tough.

Football prepares you for football; fighting prepares you for fighting. And the best way to build core toughness—the ability to take blow after blow to your midsection—is to have someone deliver blow after blow to your midsection.

A lot of my training involved standing still while Pit delivered a barrage of kicks to my midsection. But the most ridiculous drill had me doing situps, only every time my back hit the floor, Pit would beat on my midsection, my stomach, my obliques, with a giant pad.

This was in no way fun, but it sure as hell builds your tolerance for both violent collisions and the pain that accompanies them.

I remember how nervous I was the first time I stepped onto the field at Michigan Stadium—the "Big House." There were over 106,000 people there to see us play Colorado, including my parents, who had flown in for the occasion.

I was even more nervous the first time I got into an NFL game—maybe 35 seconds of garbage time against the Vikings—right up until the moment the ball was snapped. Then I could relax; I was just playing football again.

I experienced some of those same feelings on the ride to my fight. Maybe more so. Unlike in football, which I'd played for years, I was going into battle with only five training sessions under my belt.

But I was also aware of a very different feeling. The idea that I might actually get my ass kicked in a fight brought out a kind of passion and energy that I wasn't necessarily used to—what Pit called "unleashing the tiger inside."

I just hoped that I actually had a tiger inside. As the fight's promoter,

Mr. Pong, joked to the film crew, "Sometimes a lion in practice turns out, on fight night, to be a pig."

The little arena where I fought didn't have anywhere near the crowd or energy of Lumpinee Stadium, but I was still feeling the adrenaline. Pit wrapped my hands and rubbed me down with Namman Muay, a sort of Thai Bengay that feels like jalapeño peppers on your skin. I put on the traditional *mongkhon,* a headband that looks kind of like one of those novelty invisible dog leashes, worn backwards, and entered the ring to perform the ritual *wai khru* dance. Pit had spent a good part of our final training session teaching me the dance, which involves bowing three times to pay respect to the Buddha and one's teachers, trainers, and ancestors. It's the fighters' way of acknowledging that what is about to happen isn't just about them in this particular moment in time: It's about all the people and forces—alive, dead, or divine—that have brought them to this place.

As is the tradition, live musicians provided a soundtrack for the fight, playing flutes, horns, bells, and a pounding drum that is as much a part of the competition as the competition itself. Muay Thai isn't like boxing, where a jacked-up fighter might hear the opening bell and explode out of his corner. It's more of a process. During the first round, the drums go *doo . . . doo . . . doo . . . doo* as the fighters mostly feel one another out, calculating the distance each one wants to keep from the other. In the second round, it's *doo-doo . . . doo-doo . . . doo-doo,* building in intensity along with the fight. The third round sounds like an EKG monitoring a heart attack—*doodoodoodoo-doodoodoodoo*—as it whips the crowd into a frenzy, inspiring the fighters to go all out.

My fight never reached the third round. Both the promoters and my producers wanted to see me fight someone roughly my own size. The Thai may be large in spirit, but not so much in physical size; there weren't too many big guys to choose from. The one they picked—let's just be honest here—hadn't had the benefit of the same kind of athletic training and conditioning that I'd had.

I took a couple of punches, which still hurt like hell (even with the headgear that we were both wearing), but mostly it was me pounding on him with an intensity he wasn't really prepared to experience.

At the start of the second round, Pit told me to focus on my opponent's legs, which I did, unleashing kick after kick onto his shins and calves. I finally knocked him down, and when he didn't seem too eager to get up, the referee called the match.

Although it was the third episode we filmed, the Travel Channel ultimately chose it as the first one to air. Not only did it have the most color and vibrancy, but it also set a certain tone for the show. Yeah, this guy is a professional football player, but he's really doing it. He's really training that hard and he's really going to fight.

Flying out of Bangkok, I honestly felt like I had fought and won—not only the literal fight itself, but the more metaphorical (yet also very literal) battle of the bugs. I had arrived in Thailand unsure of myself and what I had thought to be my mission. As I left, I was sure that I was on the correct path.

Optimus Prime Ain't Shit without Bumblebee

Sometimes I look at a crazy person in the street and think, *I know how he got there.*

There are times you can't get out of your own head. For me, it starts to happen when my life becomes too routine. I start leading a cyclical lifestyle on the outside, which brings about cyclical thinking on the inside. I start to get lost in the voices. Or, worse, one voice starts to take over, eliminating my ability to hear the rest of them.

I'm not the only person with nine or 10 personalities. I just acknowledge them.

There are a lot of people out there who don't. They shun the voices they don't want to hear, or use drugs and alcohol to starve them until they die. But when you're killing a part of yourself, you're killing yourself, slowly but surely.

Acknowledge your personalities and feed them all that they need. It's how we grow, how we transform.

The Transformers may have been just toys, but even they were wise enough to know this truth: Optimus Prime was tough, but he wasn't shit without Bumblebee. The brain's no good without the feet. One might be able to survive without the other, but when they're all working together, good things will happen.

Mastering the Routine

(Singapore)

DRAGON BOAT RACING

The Chinese zodiac consists of 12 signs, just like the Western version. Unlike the Western version, all the Chinese signs correspond to real animals—except for one: the Dragon. The Chinese have revered dragons since ancient times, believing that they ruled the skies and provided rain for their crops. Even today, the dragon is a symbol of strength and virility.

For over 2,000 years, the Chinese have raced longboats, decorated with the head and tail of a dragon, powered by rowers whose strokes are synchronized by the beat of a drum. Some scholars believe the races were a way to pay homage to dragon gods, possibly involving human sacrifice; others claim that they originated as a way to remember Qu Yuan, a great warrior-poet who drowned himself in a river to protest a corrupt government. Whatever its origins, dragon boat racing is still popular today in China, in nearby countries with large Chinese populations, and, increasingly, all over the world.

While the original dragon boats might have been powered by several dozen paddlers, today's crews generally consist of 10 to 20 rowers, a helmsman to steer, and a drummer to keep the rowers in sync. Unlike in many other competitive rowing sports, where paddlers face the back of the boat and pull the oars toward themselves in a circular fashion, dragon boat racers face forward, requiring a sophisticated stroke that combines torso rotation with powerful shoulder strokes. Even the slightest error, whether in the stroke's form or in its timing, can create a domino effect that will slow down the entire boat. Every stroke is critical in order to win a race, some of which go longer than a mile.

We had originally hoped to film our next episode in China, the birthplace of dragon boat racing. But when we had trouble obtaining the necessary permissions, we settled on Singapore, where the large population of ethnic Chinese had carried over the sport that they loved.

This meant we'd be participating in an event that was only 22 years old instead of 2,200, but hey, that's Singapore.

POSTCARD FROM SINGAPORE

Everything is new about Singapore, an island that has only been an independent nation since 1965. It's clean, so clean that you can lick the sidewalks. I guess it helps that litterers are punished with lashes from a cane.

The people in Singapore seem more logical than creative— don't ask a cab driver to take a shortcut unless you want to confuse him. Maybe it takes a century or two for a country to develop its own artistic sensibility and temperament.

But that doesn't mean Singapore isn't a fascinating place. It's all about faces and races: Indians, Malaysians, Filipinos, and Chinese, jam-packed on an island that has over 77,000 millionaires. Where else can you buy exotic herbs in Chinatown, eat curry in Little India, and smoke a hookah (which they call a shisha in the Arab Quarter), all in just one night?

The experience in Thailand left us feeling like we knew what we were doing. Our goal in Singapore was to replicate the experience.

So I learned the sport, working out with the local champions. They weren't about to let me slow them down in a real match, but we latched on to an American team who had travelled there to race in an international competition.

I sampled strange foods, like frogs, chosen from a live tank like lobsters (think the dark meat from a chicken crossed with halibut), and the durian, a fruit with an absolutely terrible odor (it's against the law to eat them in many public spaces) that permeated my fingers. The smell is best removed, ironically enough, by washing one's hands in the empty husk of the fruit itself.

I did weird things that took me out of my comfort zone, like kampong fish therapy, where you stick your feet into a tank of thousands of tiny, toothless fish who attack your skin like it's a Sunday buffet. I got a blessing at a Hindu temple. I did my football workouts with Tim every morning, but I allowed myself to break curfew once or twice to experience a little nightlife.

The show was, it seemed, becoming a science.

The dragon boat workouts were hard as hell—football is all about training your muscles for fast-twitch, explosive movement, a completely different kind of strength from the endurance needed to paddle like a machine for 5 minutes straight or to practice 1,000 strokes in a single session—but I pushed through the pain. I helped the American team win its first heat and make the semifinals, and, while we didn't win the competition, we all celebrated as if we had.

Maybe this show wasn't going to be so hard after all.

Row, Row, Row Your Boat

Rowing is fantastic exercise, strengthening your upper body and increasing your wind while burning hundreds of calories. It's just not a particularly good exercise from a football perspective. Football players don't want to waste their workouts on building endurance—we want what Tim calls "work capacity," the ability to move with explosive strength and speed, over and over again.

We don't jog; we sprint. We don't do repetitive exercises to build the kind of muscles that will help us run marathons or carry a load for hours; we power-lift, working toward the quick first step that will let us blast out of a three-point stance, the fast-twitch muscles that will allow us to slam into an opposing player with the force of a car.

Or so I thought.

The week after Singapore, Tim and I noticed that my football lifts had improved. He was especially surprised. After 20 years of working with athletes, Tim was pretty sure he'd developed a solid system. He hadn't expected the rowing to improve my upper-body strength, at least not in football terms, yet here I was, lifting with more explosive force than I had before.

Tim likes to talk about "modalities," the idea that athletes train better—improving in all areas while avoiding the stress that comes with overtraining in one—when they are exposed to different types of exercise. He just hadn't expected the rowing modality to improve my football.

The more you do, the more you become.

The Apeshit Switch

A NOTE FROM TIM ADAMS, TRAINER

Dhani, he's got this "apeshit switch." And you don't want to be around it. Once that gets flipped, it's not a pretty sight. It's dangerous. Not just for him, but for those around him.

Everybody has an apeshit switch. A breaking point. A crazy place where the circuit breaker in your head overloads, jamming every emotion except anger. I remember a time in college when one of my teammates, an offensive lineman, kept messing around with me. The next thing I knew, I'd ripped his facemask right off his helmet.

If I let this Angry Guy come and be the front guy, I would not be where I am today. He's the reason why my father spent so much time, when I was younger, teaching me how to better understand who I am and how to moderate that part of my personality, feeding him without allowing him to take control.

Eating Sawdust
(Switzerland)

The first thing I realized about Switzerland was that there weren't any black people.

No black people. I've heard there are a few expats living somewhere in the country, and there is apparently a growing African population. I just didn't see it.

I'm used to feeling like a stranger in strange lands, but Switzerland was the first place I've been where I really felt like an alien.

POSTCARD FROM SWITZERLAND

Switzerland is a very homey place—as long as your home is Switzerland. The people weren't the warmest I've met, at least not toward me. But they're a proud people, and they've got plenty to be proud of—the country is clean, efficient, and beautiful, and has about a tenth of the crime that America does.

They love their heritage. They love their fondue. They love to yodel. Seriously. I went to a yodeling concert the night before my match. Thousands of people. Felt like Woodstock, except that what seemed freaky to me—the music, the costumes, the intensity—wasn't about breaking from conventions, but celebrating them.

SCHWINGEN

At first glance, it hardly seems like a sport: Men, generally very large men, dressed in *schwinghosen*—wrestling breeches that live somewhere between short shorts and cargo pants—grab hold of one another by the waistband, each trying to pull the other down onto a floor covered in sawdust.

But *schwingen*—from the German word for "to swing"—is Switzerland's national sport (or is at least on par with *hornussen*, a uniquely Swiss mash-up of baseball and golf, and *steinstossen*, competitive stone throwing). It's over 200 years old but comes from a much older tradition of folk wrestling, a kind of blue-collar take on the sport favored by butchers, lumberjacks, and other burly tradesmen who were more about size, strength, and attitude than formal technique.

The bouts take place in a circular ring covered in sawdust, where each wrestler tries to pin the other's shoulders to the ground while holding on to his pants. It's all about the pants: While fighters use holds, trips, and throws that resemble judo, most of the grappling involves grabbing the opponent by the back of his schwinghosen. There are referees who award points for various moves and takedowns.

Most schwingen competitions take place at festivals—sort of like state fairs, but even more popular—where each wrestler battles six or eight opponents over the course of a day. The two highest point-scorers meet in a final, but all the participants get prizes. The Swiss are big on maintaining the sport's purity, so none of the prizes involve cash: The winner is traditionally awarded a young bull; others get everything from kitchen appliances to bedroom sets. Schwingen won't make you rich, but it's not uncommon for a fighter to furnish his entire home with the spoils of his sport.

I'm not always on time.

I know it's a cliché, a black man who's not always on time you know, "C.P.T." It's not like I *can't* be on time when I have to be. I'm always early to my games and practices. I don't miss flights. But when my schedule is more relaxed, allowing me a little extra time to flow from one activity to another, I tend to be more relaxed.

Switzerland is always on time. Another cliché, I know, but everything happens like clockwork. If something is supposed to start at 8:00 p.m., you'd better be there at 7:59:59 if you don't want to miss it.

My mentor/guide was a guy named Hans. I liked Hans, even though we occasionally had trouble communicating. The Swiss have four official languages. None of them are English. To his credit, Hans knew a few words. His favorites seemed to be "But you must!"

I'm generally very humble when it comes to language differences. Travel the world and it seems like most of the people you meet speak *at least* two or three languages. Like most Americans, I struggle with one. Still, there was something about hearing those particular words that stirred the rebellious youth who still lives inside me, the one who wanted to reply, "Hell no, I don't!"

"But you must! But you must!"

Or: "This is not the way we do things!"

Or: "Oh yes, you have to!"

I think it's fair to say that there were elements to Switzerland that put me on edge.

Did I mention that there weren't any black people?

Schwingen is an old sport, a link to Switzerland's rural past. It reminded me a little of a rodeo, only the men involved weren't trying to wrestle bulls into submission, but one another. Like rodeo, there was something about the sport that felt a little bit backwoods. A little bit country.

When I walked into my first practice, I felt a very definite vibe. It wasn't "Welcome, stranger!" It was more like "Who is this guy walking in here, thinking he can play our sport?"

Fine by me. This is what competitors do to psych each other out. But I didn't feel like I was getting psyched out—I was getting *checked* out.

This might not register with the ladies, but the men all know that there's a certain etiquette to public nudity. We keep our eyes on our own urinals, if you will.

When I dropped my trousers in the schwingen locker room, it was all eyes on me. I'm not talking about a subtle glance out of the corner of an eye. These guys were blatantly staring at my dick.

I started to feel like a very black man at a very white country club. "He speaks so well!" I could imagine people saying. "Jenny, you should go talk to him! Mary, Susan, you really should have a conversation with Dhani. He has fabulous diction."

I tried to erase those thoughts from my mind as I pulled up my schwinghosen—which felt a lot like a loincloth—and made my way to the practice area.

The fights take place in a sawdust pit, providing a little cushion for when you get knocked on the ground. Which happened to me with my very first opponent—he grabbed me by the britches and slammed me face-first into the floor.

No reason to panic. I wrestled in high school. I get knocked down all the time on the football field. I knew exactly what to do: Take a deep breath and get back up.

Only when I took a deep breath, I wasn't inhaling air. My mouth and throat filled with sawdust. I coughed, choked, and struggled to clear my throat. As soon as I could pull myself off the ground, I ran back to the locker room and washed out my mouth.

I returned to the sawpit. I looked at Hans, who seemed to be saying, *Get back in there!* I looked at my smiling producers. *Wow! This is great TV! Let's get some more of this!*

Didn't anybody notice that I almost suffocated in there?

No time to feel sorry for myself—the next guy was on me. This time I was ready. I threw him on the floor.

Before I could celebrate, another guy was on me. Then another. Now I could feel a definite vibe in the room. The coach was yelling at his fighters to "Go! Go! Go!" The fighters had a look in their eyes, like they were pitting themselves against a beast. *Let's see how strong this black guy really is!*

Maybe I was imagining the whole thing . . .

Maybe if I stopped to think about it . . .

But I didn't have time to stop and think about it. The opponents kept coming at me like I was in a Bruce Lee movie.

I looked at Hans. He seemed to be aware of what was going on, but this was his crew. He wasn't about to side with me against them.

I looked at my producers. They were smiling, watching "good TV" become "great TV." I clearly wasn't going to get any help from them.

I could almost hear the *click* of the apeshit switch going off in my head.

All right then. This is schwingen? It's time to swing. Even if I've got to kill a motherfucker.

A NOTE FROM TIM ADAMS, TRAINER

The reason I stopped the fight? Part of it was protecting Dhani. But really, part of it was protecting those other guys. It was just like, "He's flipped, and we need to stop. Now."

I don't know how many guys I fought before Tim stepped in and stopped the fight. At least eight. Tim says it was more like 18.

A little while later, after I'd had a chance to calm down, I went upstairs and had a beer with Hans.

The vibe had changed. A few minutes earlier, Hans had been the enemy. Now we were cool. We were friends. I understood how difficult his sport was, and he saw that I could take the punishment. We'd moved into a place of mutual respect.

Practice was easier after that. I competed in a tournament at the end of the week, and I did pretty well, winning a couple of matches. I don't know that I actually got a standing ovation, but it felt like one to me. I'd earned some respect.

Maybe it was all in my head. Maybe it was all in theirs. More likely, it was all of us.

So the show wasn't quite a science. I realized that every country was going to have a different personality. I was (and still am) learning the way, perfecting the technique of immersing myself in a new culture, being respectful of the people and the journey.

My producers and I were also developing a relationship. I understood their desire for great TV. But I do all my own stunts. Every hit I take, that's me getting hit. That guy suffocating because of the sawdust in his mouth? That's me.

We were going to make mistakes. But we were also figuring out how to adapt to them more quickly. No matter how difficult the equation might be, you go into it with the same mind. We were learning how to learn.

A NOTE FROM JONATHAN FIERRO, PRODUCER

The good thing about Dhani, you can have a blowup with him, and the next day it's like, "Okay, that was yesterday."

I think our first blowup came, appropriately enough, in Ireland. We couldn't agree on the best way to pronounce

"Corke Park" and almost got into a shoving match. But that wasn't bad. It was more like fun. Because once you push Dhani and he pushes you back, you don't really get to push back again. It's like, "Okay, I just got knocked out. Cool! Let's talk about this a little bit later!"

THE UPSIDE OF APESHIT

Let your Angry Guy control your personality, and be prepared to face some potentially detrimental consequences. But the Angry Guy can also be your friend, if you treat him right and establish the appropriate boundaries.

The guys I had to fight in Switzerland were much bigger than me. Some of them were 270 pounds, country-bred white boys straight off a farm where they baled hay, lifted cows, and knocked down trees with their foreheads all day. I knew it was going to take a certain kind of energy to compete with them. It's a little like the feel-good space we talked about earlier: If you want to make real gains in your life, you're going to have to put yourself in uncomfortable situations. Places where you feel like you're outnumbered or unliked. Where the people around you are stronger than you, know more than you, can do it better than you can.

Survive that space—slay the dragon, if you will—and you will find yourself in a stronger place than you were before.

In Switzerland, I prepared myself for my fights by walking alone in a field. I meditated on the circuit box in my head, figuring out which breakers had tripped—and which needed to be reset—and "got my mind right," leaving fear and uncertainty behind.

You can do this in your own life. For example, before you go to the gym, take 5 minutes to sit by yourself, analyzing what it is you want to attain. Then take another 5 minutes to think about all the things that scare you, all the people who are further along than you are, all the reasons why you are going to fail.

Find your apeshit switch. Turn it on. Use it to demolish all those fears. Then shut it off and go to the gym.

When you're ready to lift that previously unliftable weight, or push yourself to go an extra 5 minutes on your run, flip that switch back on. You might be amazed at what you can accomplish.

Just remember to turn it off afterwards.

Black Man

I was recently in Beirut, Lebanon, a city that gets a bad rap. Yes, there are bullet holes in most of the buildings. But walk the streets for a few minutes and you'll see guys wearing Armani blazers, rocking Gucci loafers, sporting $250,000 Piagets. There are Porsches and Ferraris and rooftop pools where people pop bottles of Cristal and lounge on beds that rotate 360 degrees to get the best view of the Mediterranean. It's the San Francisco of the Middle East, pulling in the party people from Saudi Arabia, Kuwait, Iran, and Iraq.

I was hanging out with my friend Jason at a place called Beiruf that, as the name suggests, is at the top of a building. The scene was not so different from any urban club-of-the-moment. Beautiful women dancing. Men trying to get their attention. Reggae superstar Shaggy partying with his entourage at a private table.

At the end of the night, we got into the down elevator with two girls. But before the doors could close, two more guys jumped in, members of Shaggy's entourage.

The elevator said "overload." But at 2:00 in the morning, everybody's puffing out their chests. Nobody's getting off the elevator. Jason and I felt like we had first dibs. Shaggy's crew felt like it was their birthright. "Rastifari, mon!" they yelled. "Big ups to Brooklyn!"

"Big ups to Brooklyn? Come on, now. This is Beirut, man. Brooklyn hasn't seen a mortar since the Revolutionary War. A few drive-bys, maybe, but no paratroopers, no tanks, no missiles."

Two o'clock in the morning, in an elevator with Shaggy's henchmen, yelling, cussing, confirming for the world every negative stereotype of the Black American.

Moral of the story? It was the girls who got off the elevator.

I have a couple of cars, but my favorite is my Mini Cooper. People aren't necessarily used to seeing a black man drive a Mini Cooper—especially other black men. But every once in a while, I'll get a nod from a brother, as in, *That's a sweet car.*

Maybe he's never seen another black man driving an English car. Maybe he's thinking, *I've got to get something different from the Impala, the Cadillac, the Chrysler 300, the Mercedes. I'm going to learn about English cars. Maybe I'm going to get a Mini Cooper, an MG, or a Morgan.*

Maybe he's seen me on TV. A black man travelling in a foreign country, eating weird foods, doing some different shit. Maybe the idea of travelling the world is going to creep into his thought process. Maybe he's developing a new idea of what is acceptable, cool, or possible.

Black people don't travel? I'm travelling all the time. Black people don't swim, ride bikes, do martial arts, or eat strange foods? Watch my show. Black men can't be president? Check out the White House.

Yes, they can. Yes, they do. Yes, they will.

You can be proud of your heritage, proud of your culture, proud of where you come from, and still be a chameleon just like everybody else. You don't have to buy into the propaganda, the stereotypes, or the shortfalls people put before you.

Just open up your eyes and think about yourself as a human being instead of limiting yourself as a race. Everybody can be everything.

Expectations vs. Reality
(Spain)

I n Switzerland, I was dealing with other people's prejudices. In the Basque region of Spain, where I went to learn jai alai, I had to deal with my own prejudgment.

Bombs.

That's the first word that popped into my head when I heard the word "Basque." Forty years of kidnappings and car bombs, the modern incarnation of a nearly 200-year struggle for autonomy from Spanish rule. I was imagining a place where one misstep, one misstatement, the wrong place at the wrong time, and I was going to end up dead.

Sometimes stereotypes are based in reality. The Irish love whiskey. Thailand really does have Ping-Pong shows. Singapore gives lashes to litterers. Everybody in Switzerland is white. Almost everybody, anyway.

But the stereotypes don't define a person or place. They're shortcuts. They're lazy. Maybe it was because I felt like I'd been on the receiving end in Switzerland, but I told myself that when I got to Spain, I was going to erase my own stereotypes. Yes, I was aware of the political climate. But I had to overcome all that if I wanted to see the culture.

POSTCARD FROM SPAIN

The Basque region of Spain is one of the most beautiful places on God's earth. And the people know exactly whom to thank— there are churches everywhere. Morality is important to the people. You want to meet a young lady, you'd better talk to her like a well-intentioned gentleman does, and do it during the day—at night you're going to seem like a predator.

But they don't let morality get in the way of enjoying life. The men cook and serve gourmet meals at txoko, *gastronomic societies where they laugh, drink, and talk about everything— except politics. It's forbidden. Too serious. There's an art to pouring* txakoli, *the local sparkling wine, and it's poured often. The people love to gamble, especially on jai alai. Kids run naked on the beaches. Everyone naps in the afternoon.*

It's a magical place for people who love to love life.

Technically speaking, the Basque region is part of Spain, but it's about as similar to Barcelona as Dublin is to Belfast. The Basque have their own language, cuisine, and customs, and many of them bristle if you call them "Spaniards."

Despite my preconceptions, however, politics seemed very far away. Unlike Ireland, where it never seemed to take much to trigger an emotional debate about the North-South conflict, the Basque people I met were much more interested in talking about wine, culture, jai alai, and food.

The food . . .

I'd eaten a lot of interesting things during my travels, which mainly were just that: interesting. I could endure it and even enjoy it (most of the time, anyway), but none of it was going to change what I thought was a fundamental fact about me: I don't like to eat. I have a few comfort staples—grapes, oatmeal raisin cookies, vanilla ice cream, Twinkies, and Sprite—but I grew up eating to live, not living to eat. My mother says I treat food like an anorexic schoolgirl. She can't believe that I'm able to keep up my weight.

Everything changed in San Sebastián. Maybe I'd just developed an appetite after more than a month on the road. Maybe I was just grateful not to be eating frogs and bugs. Maybe it was the open-minded attitude I'd sworn to adopt. Whatever it was, I started eating like an entirely different person.

After every jai alai practice, I'd go out with my teammates for *chuleta,* the biggest, baddest, most savory steak I've ever had. I'm talking about the Fred Flintstone cut, infused with smoke. Makes me hungry just thinking about it.

Then there were the *pintxos,* little dishes that you'd better not call tapas—those are for the Spanish. Anchovies, shredded pork, chorizo, olives. The flavors were incredible.

Even the simple meals seemed to have some magical quality to them. Grilled fish and potatoes tasted like they'd been prepared by the world's greatest gourmet chef. I ate, washed it down with sangria or txakoli, and ate some more.

The effects of my visit are still with me today. I love food! To hell with McDonald's—bring on the *petit filet, rareplus, s'il vous plaît.* Or a dozen Kumamoto oysters with a wedge of lemon. I'll go a mile out of my way for tarte tatin. I'll fly to New York City after a game just to get some good sushi.

A NOTE FROM DR. NANCY JONES

Finally. If it takes him travelling the globe to learn how to eat, so be it.

JAI ALAI

During medieval times, villagers would often gather outside churches for holiday festivals. Churches tend to have high walls. Spend enough time around a high wall, and it's only a matter of time until someone starts throwing a ball against it. And so began jai alai, a Basque phrase for "merry festival."

Perhaps influenced by their northern neighbors, the French— whose *jeu de palme* (handball) evolved into modern tennis—the Basque realized they could make the ball go a lot faster if they used some kind of racquet. They eventually came up with the cesta, a basket made from chestnut wood that gets soaked and dried for months before it's carefully hand-planed and woven into shape.

The cesta didn't just make the ball go faster—it made the ball go a shit-ton faster. The pelota regularly reaches speeds of nearly 200 miles an hour. The three walls of the court, or *cancha*—front, back, and left— are generally made of granite, as the rock-hard pelota travels with enough force to shatter bulletproof glass.

Players have to catch the ball cleanly, after one bounce or on the fly, and return it against the front wall in one fluid motion; mess up, and the other team gets a point. The first player or team (jai alai can be played one-on-one or two-on-two) to get to seven points wins.

Not surprisingly, people have died playing this game, which is nicknamed "the ballet of bullets." Today's jai alai players wear helmets to protect their heads from the pelota. What is surprising is that most deaths don't come from ball-related injuries, but heart attacks. No one is sure whether it's the excitement of the game or the repeated stress of stretching the chest cavity to hurl the ball down a 175-foot court.

STRETCHING (WITHOUT DYING)

There isn't any workout that will prepare you for jai alai. Truth is, the game is more a skill than a sport, a lesson I learned when my partner

Miguel and I lost a practice match to a couple of 7-year-olds. My so-called strength and athleticism didn't help me a lick.

That being said, I did notice that the game stretched my body in ways that felt new to me. My chest cavity seemed to expand; my shoulders broadened. If you don't happen to have a cesta and pelota on hand, you can approximate the motion by standing with your feet spread shoulder-width apart, straightening your arms to full extension at your sides, and twisting your entire head and torso back and forth in a semicircular motion.

You'll literally be opening up your heart.

———

While jai alai turned out to be the least physically demanding sport on my trip, I was grateful for the change of pace. The episode wound up focusing more on the food and culture than on the game or my preparation. Miguel and I won our match at the end of the show, but it wasn't because of anything I did. Or, better said, we won *despite* anything I did—Miguel is a world-class jai alai star.

But a win is a win any day. I was happy to take it.

———

A NOTE FROM JONATHAN FIERRO, PRODUCER

I think you'll always, with the host of a show, use a little bit of a filter. Jai alai is a crazy sport, the ball moving at who-knows-what speed off these walls, and it's all hand-eye coordination. Then Dhani went out and did body boarding with one of the guys on the team, and he got bashed in the lip by some kid's surfboard. I mean, like a grapefruit on his lip. We let him rest for the remainder of the day.

The next day, he's like, "How does it look?"

"It looks great!" I told him. "You can't even see it!"

Then I whispered to Andre, the cameraman, "Let's just shoot Dhani from the side today."

That's right: With all the fears I had heading in, the greatest danger in Spain wasn't bombs, but boards. Had I been in the States, I probably would have gone to the hospital for stitches.

Forty days on the road. I'd survived rugby and hurling, eight-limbed fighters and folk-wrestling Goliaths. Even jai alai, a game nicknamed "the dance of death." But it was a damn surfboard that wound up hurting the most.

Learning to Talk about It

I was lucky to have my trainer, Tim, along on my travels. He made sure I woke up every morning at 5:00 or 6:00 to keep me doing what I had to do to stay prepared for my day job with the Bengals. He was also incredibly creative at finding ways to use whatever training I had to do for a particular sport in a way that enhanced or replaced aspects of my football workouts. Every day he'd look at what I was doing, I'd tell him how I was feeling, and he'd come up with a plan.

Tim knew I'd be ready to play football. I knew I'd be ready to play football. The question was, Would the coaches and ownership believe that I was ready to play football?

I was back on that island, hoping to cross the bridge back to my team. There wasn't going to be any bridge if people thought I was too distracted to play the game.

So Tim didn't just tailor my training—he also taught me how to tailor my mind-set. Whenever anyone asked me a question about my summer "vacation," I'd answer it in a way that demonstrated how all of the "distractions" were helping me to become a better football player.

"Muay Thai boxing is an extremely focused form of exercise for my back muscles, stomach muscles, core strength, and stability."

"Dragon boat racing builds upper-body strength and wind capacity while allowing my leg muscles to rest and recover."

"Schwingen is grappling, teaching me how to tackle opponents more efficiently."

"Jai alai improves lateral quickness and upper-body flexibility."

With every question I was asked, I became a little bit more intelligent about how to communicate what I was doing in a way that assured people that football was always my true focus.

It hardly occurred to me that I might actually be telling the truth.

Back to Camp

A NOTE FROM DON YEE, AGENT

If you do something for a long time, the hope is that, if you're reasonably aware, you'll develop some good instincts and judgment. No one else could see it or understand it yet, but it was very clear to me: Dhani was going to be a great fit for the Bengals.

Marvin Lewis, head coach of the Bengals, had a very poor defense. A very young defense. He also had a very poor locker room dynamic. They were losers, basically. And had been losers for a long time.

I felt that number one, Dhani and Marvin would connect on a personal level. They're both intelligent guys. They're both facile with the English language. And they're both verbose.

Number two, Dhani had been in places where he had won, so he knew what it was like to be around a winning team and what a winning locker room looks like. I felt that he could contribute there.

Number three, the Bengals had not had a productive, smart, and grounded middle linebacker, a Mike backer, in a long time. It's a big job because, essentially, you are the quarterback of the defense. Apart from understanding the entire defense and everybody's assignments, and being able to communicate with your defensive coordinator and make the calls on the field, you have to be able to lead. You have to be able to nurture. And I felt that even though Dhani hadn't played the position since college, he could make the transition. I just felt that he was at the right age, at the right time, to be that kind of emotional glue.

The Bengals were skeptical. Dhani was skeptical. But I felt that he could do it quite easily if given the opportunity.

Two days after I returned from Spain to Cincinnati, training camp began. The grinding ritual of two-a-day practices in the summer sun. The time for your body to tell you the absolute truth about where you are.

I blasted through it.

Part of it was a psychological game I play with myself: Everybody's looking at me, thinking about the way I spent my off-season, waiting to see me drag, waiting for me to get injured. If I get tired, if I develop a nagging injury, I can't do all the other stuff.

To hell with that. I'm not getting tired. Travelling the world didn't wear me down—it energized me.

Part of it was a sense of relief: I tend to be very detail-oriented, which can leave me feeling scattered. Forty days on the road meant moving from one place to another, constantly changing my schedule, my diet, my focus. Now it was time for football. Time to flip the master switch. Can't divert any energy away from the main circuit, so everything else goes away.

It's easy when every day is the same. Wake up at the same time I did yesterday. Walk from my room to the training room, the training room to the locker room, the locker room to the field. Play football. Back through the locker room to the training room to the weight room to the ice tub to my room for some sleep. Repeat.

Part of it was a rebirth: I'd spent the past several years feeling out of sorts, like I wasn't meeting expectations; my job was insecure. But the Bengals had made a commitment to me. They didn't just want me to play—they wanted me to lead.

That spring, the team drafted Keith Rivers, a highly regarded linebacker out of USC who played weak side linebacker, the Will.

My position.

I experienced a brief moment of "here we go again," until Coach Lewis explained that I wasn't getting pushed out the door—I was being invited inside. We had a new defensive coordinator, Mike Zimmer, who wanted to give me a shot at playing the Mike—middle linebacker—the defensive version of the quarterback.

I wasn't fired; I was getting a promotion.

So there were a lot of reasons to explain why I was blasting through camp. Part of it, however, came as a complete surprise. I wasn't tired because I wasn't tired. My body felt great. My mind was refreshed. Deep in my soul, I knew I was ready for football.

And for that, I had to credit my off-season.

Coach Lewis set the tone for the 2008 season with a single word: "Now."

But sometimes now has to wait for later.

Our quarterback, Carson Palmer, wound up missing most of the season with an elbow injury. Our leading rusher had signed elsewhere during the off-season, and we didn't find someone who could fill his shoes until the fifth week of the season. The defense was rebuilding under Mike Zimmer, but there were clearly going to be some growing pains.

We lost our first eight games. The Bengals had missed the playoffs for the third straight year.

But it wasn't all hopeless. We went 4-3-1 over the second half of the season. In fact, we finished with three straight wins, shutting out our opponents for the final seven quarters of the season. I adapted quickly to the Mike and, from a statistical standpoint, had what was arguably the best year of my career.

Iterations

Some people see life as the proverbial hamster wheel. No matter how hard we run, we keep coming back to the same place.

I feel like I'm always coming around to the same place. My college football career took me from Will to Sam to Mike. The pros? Will to Sam to Mike.

Senior year of high school: career in jeopardy (bad back). Five years later, with the Giants: career in jeopardy (bad knee). Five years later, with the Eagles: career in jeopardy (bad performance).

It goes deeper than that. People I know, the relationships I enter, everything always seems to come around to where it was before. The wheel keeps spinning.

All that said, life is not a hamster wheel. The situations may stay the same, but the hamster is always changing.

Every night we sleep, we dream, and in a sense, we die. Morning comes, and there's nothing that says we have to be the same person we were the night before.

Look up the word "iteration." The first definition is usually something like "repetition." But it's almost always followed by a second definition along the lines of "repetition until a desired result is achieved."

Life is a karmic wheel. No matter how much things seem the same, we keep evolving.

Yes, I Can Swim
(Australia)

SURF LIFESAVING

Australia has a reputation as rugged country, but locals will tell you that most of its dangers lie just off its shores. The surrounding ocean is home to the box jellyfish, the blue ring octopus, and the stonefish, three of the most venomous creatures in the world. Many beaches are surrounded by shark nets, protecting swimmers from the great whites that hunt in the area. The surf itself is often violent—it's not uncommon to see 12-foot waves—and sudden rip currents can pull even the most experienced swimmers out to sea.

A little over a hundred years ago, Australia's beach communities began organizing groups of volunteers called "surf lifesavers." These men were trained to protect, rescue, and, when necessary, revive swimmers, using ropes, buoys, and peak physical fitness.

Today there are more than 300 surf lifesaving clubs. Still wholly manned by volunteers, they rescue nearly 10,000 people each year. While the methods have evolved—modern surf lifesavers use specially designed rescue boards, Jet Skis, kayaks, and helicopters—the old ways are still respected and celebrated. Surf lifesaving competitions have grown into one of Australia's favorite sports.

Local surf clubs battle against one another in a carnival atmosphere, demonstrating their endurance, stamina, and reflexes. Events include beach sprints and "flags" (a race and scrum to retrieve a small length of rubber hose), competitive board paddles and double-ski races, and, of course, an ocean swim. In recent years, the sport has increased in popularity, inspiring similar competitions in the United States, Canada, and Europe.

I'd heard great things about Australia. I'd also heard some things that were not so great. *Australians don't like black people. Look at the way they treat the Aborigines there.*

But my mission is always to wipe the slate clean. Forget about the preconceptions and the stereotypes, and experience a place through new eyes.

A NOTE FROM JONATHAN FIERRO, PRODUCER

We're shooting Dhani in Australia, and some guy leans over to me and says, "Hey, can he swim? You sure you want to put him in as a surf lifesaver?" The guy was being genuine. I don't know if he just didn't know, but sometimes that's what it's like when you're travelling with a black TV host.

Okay, so maybe there was a little racism. Subtle stuff like "This is sand, Dhani. Do you know how to run in sand? Are you sure you know how to swim?"

I've been in pools since I was 8 months old. When I was 12, I was one of the top breaststroke swimmers in my age group. In the entire U.S. of A. Hell yes, I can swim!

There's a part of me that wants to act up in those situations. The lifesavers like to wear "budgie smugglers," or what Americans sometimes call "banana hammocks." I had a little fun wandering around a clothing store in my own form-fitting bathing suit, scaring the bejeezus out of a couple of old men.

But there's another part of me that is, dare I say, *maturing.* All the little bits and pieces I'd experienced in other countries helped me get through Australia. I like to learn from the past, adding to the checklist of things to apply to the future. I'm not a rookie traveller; I'm the savvy veteran.

POSTCARD FROM AUSTRALIA

There's no place like Australia, which is either an enormous country or a small continent. The seafood is incredible. Got to see a shark close up in a tank. Maybe saw another one in the ocean. (I'm sure I did, even if no one else believes me.)

In and around Sydney, life is a beach. Everyone is territorial, proud of their particular beach, and everybody takes care of their body, since they spend half their life in a bathing suit. Could afford to use some sunscreen, however—saw a lot of 24-year-olds who looked like 44-year-olds.

Yes, Australians have an edge to them. They are brash, arrogant, and proud of their Aussiness in a way that borders on elitism. But there's something about that mentality that is suitable to a land of bandits— after all, Australia was to England what Siberia is to Russia, a place to send society's quote-unquote undesirable elements. Maybe they still have a lingering bad taste in their mouths from being outcasts. It's built into their DNA.

And there is a certain charm to their rough hooligan ways. They like to party. Shit, they party their asses off. Maybe we're not going to hold hands and sing "Kumbaya," but we can have some fun while we're hanging out together.

And remember that surf lifesaving is a volunteer job. For these guys, saving lives is a hobby. They can't be that bad.

Dealing with the culture wasn't the only way in which I had to be a savvy veteran; I had to deal with a producer, as well. Every morning there was some reason—the best time to swim, the perfect light, a run with the lifesaving team along the beach—that required me to be someplace at 5:00 a.m. Don't you know I just finished a football season?

Then there was the shark.

During one of my training swims, I swear to God I saw a man-size shark out there. A man in a grey suit rolled past me. A grey Cadillac rolled past me.

Give me a few years to work on the story. By the time I'm 80, I will have wrestled the shark into submission with one hand behind my back so that I could rescue a group of Girl Scouts.

No one else saw that shark. But I know that I did.

I'd like to say that I swam like Jesse Owens ran in Munich, 1936, single-handedly disproving all the stereotypes. But when the competition came around, I came in last place in the 100-yard sand dash, barely completed the 600-meter ocean swim, and literally fell off the men's double-ski. The only event where I was able to make the proverbial splash was the flag race, a scramble and scrum to retrieve ribbons from the sand. It reminded me of a football fumble drill.

The surf lifesavers were a lot better at their sport than I was. But given the stakes involved in their real-life success or failure, I suppose that's a good thing. A very good thing.

GET INTO MOTION IN THE OCEAN

For a lot of people, the idea of "recovery" from some sort of strenuous activity involves sleeping through the alarm clock. Getting a massage. Lying on a beach with a piña colada in hand.

Those are all viable forms of *passive* recovery. But there's a lot of scientific evidence to suggest that the fastest way to get your body right again isn't to shut down, but to put it through a less strenuous form of exercise. Trainers call this *active* recovery.

There's some debate over the reasons why it works, but on a basic level, you're increasing the bloodflow to muscles that you've previously broken down, which may help them to recover faster. Exercise also helps increase your level of psychological relaxation, which has positive effects when it comes to recovery. So the day after I do a series of hard-core sprints, I might go for a short jog just to help keep the process moving along.

Swimming is a great form of active recovery. You're increasing the bloodflow to your muscles without causing them so much stress that they begin to break down again.

Ocean swimming may even do more than that.

You hear scientists talking more and more about "free radicals," ions with positive charges and potentially negative effects, from rapid aging to depression to cancer. We're supposedly surrounded by free radicals, which come from air pollution, radiation, and household electronics. They're the reason everybody talks about antioxidants, foods and vitamins that are supposed to battle the effects of these positively charged ions.

Another way to combat positive ions, however, is with negative ions. And ocean surf is believed to be one of the world's greatest natural producers of negative ions, which you'll breathe in while you're swimming through the waves.

I'm not qualified to get into any sort of scientific debate on the subject. But it seems like there are a lot worse things you could do for your body than getting your ass to the ocean and, assuming the water's not full of toxic sludge (or sharks), going for a swim.

Mr. Snake
(Cambodia)

The junior Einstein in me still loves physics. I can't claim to know much, but I do know that there is a relationship between the observer and the observed, and that one changes the other in ways that can be completely unpredictable.

Nowhere has that seemed clearer to me than in Phnom Penh, Cambodia. It was the reason why, as I warmed up for my pradal serey match, kids were following me down the street like I was Muhammad Ali: A black American followed by TV cameras was a massive disruption from the normal flow, one that may have prevented me from seeing the "real" Cambodia. And it's the reason I found myself in a remote Cambodian village, a live rooster in one hand, a dead chicken in the other, hoping against hope that the biggest snake I'd ever seen would eat one or both.

POSTCARD FROM CAMBODIA

Arriving there at dusk, Phnom Penh glows like a brilliant sky over the Pacific Ocean. But the illusion doesn't last for long. It starts with the first "officer" we meet, who asks us to pay a fee for some unspecified service. Then another officer. And another.

Once we've pushed through that wave, we're into the city itself. Filth and poverty are everywhere. The lucky people have motorcycles or scooters and can offer rides to tourists, so they can maybe afford to share a home or apartment. Many others sleep outside.

I couldn't wait to get to my hotel, an oasis from the despair.

But the more time I spent in Cambodia, the more generosity I experienced, the more smiles I saw. It's always good to be reminded that a place doesn't need money to be rich.

PRADAL SEREY

Pradal serey—the Khmer phrase for "free fighting"—may be the oldest form of kickboxing in the world. Over a thousand years ago, the Khmer used it to rule most of Southeast Asia. Many centuries later, French colonialists would help transform it into a sport, incorporating the Western ideas of boxing gloves, rounds, and a ring. When the Khmer Rouge took control of Cambodia in 1975—beginning a reign of terror that killed more than 20 percent of the population, specifically the most skilled and educated—they outlawed pradal serey, imprisoning or executing many of its practitioners. The sport was nearly wiped out of existence.

The Khmer Rouge were overthrown 4 years later, and the Cambodians began the process of restoring their lost arts and culture, including pradal serey. It is the country's national sport and a means for many young Cambodians to escape the poverty afflicting one of the world's least developed countries. The top fighters—who often work out all day, every day, with a coach called a *kruu*—can earn more than $100 per match.

In practice, pradal serey is very similar to Muay Thai, the martial art it helped spawn. Fighters partake in a prematch prayer ritual, and the fights are scored by live musicians. The subtle differences include more emphasis on blasting opponents with the elbows, powerful kicks that come from the hip, and the use of a "clinch," grabbing one's opponent by the neck to wear him down.

A NOTE FROM JONATHAN FIERRO, PRODUCER

What's it like to travel with a black TV host and a camera crew? In Cambodia, we got out of the van and people were yelling, "Mr. Obama! Mr. Obama! Mr. Obama!"

Getting to the gym operated by my kruu, Long Salavorn, meant travelling through some of the worst poverty I've ever seen. Naked kids running around in the streets, where traffic flowed any which way. Feral dogs. Garbage everywhere. Toilets were a state of mind—I saw people pee through the slats of their living room floors.

The "gym" also happened to be Long's family home; every morning, they'd move some beds and roll out a workout mat. I changed in their kitchen while Long's wife cooked breakfast.

Long's English wasn't very good, but it was a lot better than my Khmer, so that's what we used. But much of what we said to one another was lost in translation. Long would often disappear for long stretches of time, leaving me confused about what to do next.

When we did work out together, it was often punishing—sparring practice, pushups and core exercises, and a kruu-delivered beating to the head and midsection with a heavy pad, in a house so hot that even my toes were frothing with sweat.

Then we hit the streets for an afternoon run. The Cambodians weren't used to seeing black men or television cameras, and wherever we went, we seemed to be the main event. I don't mind being the center of attention, but it was hard not to feel a little awkward and self-indulgent in the midst of so much economic hardship.

I felt more comfortable when we got into our "tackling the globe" routine. We visited a break-dancing center where 8-year-old kids showed me what rhythm and athleticism were all about. I ate a fried tarantula—on the condition that my way-too-smug producers follow my lead. (I let them buy their way out when they turned over a secret stash of Twinkies and Sprite.) I saw a show performed by Cambodian dancer/acrobats who could fire arrows with their feet and suspend themselves on a bar, perpendicular to the ground, using only their teeth.

Weird, but cool. The day before my fight, however, things got just plain weird.

Long tried to explain, with his limited English, that I'd be doing some practice sparring with a live opponent. I tried to explain that I was cool with the idea, as long as the opponent understood that I wasn't a trained fighter and that I couldn't afford to get hurt. "Twenty percent," I kept saying. "Tell him not to go more than 20 percent."

Then I noticed that dozens of kids had gathered to watch the fight. My opponent had a look in his eye that seemed to say, "You think you're a badass, American? I'm going to show you what fighting is all about."

The TV cameras weren't going to keep me safe—in fact, their presence seemed to be changing the dynamic, spurring my opponent on. He was jumping around like he was hot shit. This was going to be his big debut, messing up some American celebrity in front of an international audience.

The first kick to my face confirmed it: I was in a real fight. I was going to have to get my mind right in a hurry.

Click.

There went the apeshit switch.

He got in a couple of good shots, but he couldn't match my size or strength. I didn't care about being polite or gracious, or displaying anything resembling cultural sensitivity. I pounded that smug look right off his face.

We didn't have too much trouble with translation after that.

One of the show's standbys was for me to dabble in a culture's more mystical practices. Most of the time it was as easy as visiting a local temple. In Cambodia, we stretched the idea a little. Or a lot: I was going to get a blessing from a magical snake.

My guide took me to a market and instructed me to buy two chickens. One live. One dead. It didn't matter that the live "chicken" was actually a rooster. The saleslady just plopped him in a plastic trash bag and sent us on our way to a remote village to meet "Mr. Snake," who, assuming he accepted my gifts, would bestow me with good luck for my fight the next day.

Mr. Snake certainly was an impressive specimen. Sixteen feet long, 265 pounds. One of the locals suggested I start with the dead chicken, which I gingerly placed in front of the beast. When Mr. Snake showed no interest, I pulled out the live rooster and did the same.

Here I was, in the middle of God-knows-where, rooting for a giant snake to eat a live rooster. What the hell was going on with me? The observer had been transformed by the observed.

I tried not to worry when Mr. Snake rejected both of my offerings.

A NOTE FROM TIM ADAMS, TRAINER

We get to the stadium where Dhani is fighting and this guy, one of the best fighters at the gym where he's been training, is sitting on a table. Wrapped up in bandages. Blood spurting out of his nose. The guy broke both orbital sockets. He had to get surgery the next day because his face was caved in. It was horrendous. And I'm telling you, I'm freaking out, just going, "Oh my gosh, what have we gotten ourselves into again?!"

It was time for my fight.

Long Salavorn was nowhere to be found. Some other trainer rubbed me down with a mysterious oil and spit water on my back—apparently a pradal serey tradition. A kid I'd never seen before wrapped my hands with tape in a way that failed to inspire confidence. I had no idea what to expect. The only thing I knew was that in a short time I'd be in a ring, fighting in a style I barely knew, against an opponent who would likely be looking to build a name for himself in front of a television camera.

I decided to escape to the streets to clear my head.

Only there was no escape. As the cameras followed me, so did Phnom Penh. People started trailing me through the streets. The growing crowd made me feel like Ali again, in Zaire, on his way to the "Rumble in the Jungle." I decided I could do worse, pulling up my sweatshirt hood and mentally preparing myself to float like a butterfly and sting like a bee. I got so focused that I barely noticed when my cameraman fell backwards into a 3-foot-deep ditch. I hoped he was going to be okay.

I hoped I was going to be okay.

I'd like to say that I put on a great show. In truth, the three-round fight was a slog. My opponent and I both landed plenty of bruising blows, but there wasn't anything graceful about it.

I'd like to say that I scored a decisive win. But when the third round ended, what seemed like a dozen judges argued for a dozen minutes about who had won. It turned out to be me.

I'd like to say that I tackled Cambodia. Maybe I did.

But you'd be just as correct in saying that Cambodia had tackled me.

NECK EXERCISES, CAMBODIAN STYLE

Football players are sometimes portrayed as having no necks. Not true. We have necks, ideally very strong necks. While it's increasingly frowned upon, many of the hits we lay on one another lead with the helmet, which is, of course, mainly supported by the neck. Having a strong neck also helps us to avoid injuries, the kinds of serious injuries that end careers . . . or worse.

There are several types of exercises that will strengthen the neck, either directly, through machines specifically designed for the purpose, or indirectly—shoulder shrugs and clean jerks with a heavy bar both help. But I've never encountered a neck exercise quite as simple or effective as the one I learned in Long Salavorn's gym.

Pradal serey fighters need strong necks to resist the clinches their opponents use to wear down their resistance. There aren't too many workout machines in Cambodia, so the fighters use what they have: a heavy weight and literally the shirt off their back.

We simply looped the shirt through the hole in the center of the weight and held it in our teeth.

Lift head up, lower head down.

Repeat until exhausted.

Brotherhood

Football is a team sport.

The idea of a team sport may inspire images of a group of people working together as one. A place where the individual plays second fiddle to the collective whole.

Which is all true—to some extent.

Football is also a competition that never ends. No one is guaranteed a job, and there is always someone who wants yours.

You might expect this cold fact to create a lot of tension among fellow football players. But more often than not, the opposite is true: Football players feel a unique camaraderie with other football players. Not just with players on their own team but with those on other teams as well, despite engaging in hand-to-hand combat with these opponents on a weekly basis.

It's all rooted in understanding. Who else is going to understand what you've had to go through to get where you are now?

When I look at another football player, I'm looking at someone who has been through a lifetime of grueling two-a-day practices. Sometimes three-a-days. Someone who's had his ass whooped. Someone who's knocked someone out. He's been cussed at by a coach. Faked someone out. Experienced the relief when an injury turns out to be nothing serious—and the grief when it does. He's won and he's lost. Made spectacular plays and been thoroughly embarrassed. Someone who has lived through a life full of tests and is still doing what he needs to do to pass them.

Maybe it's the same for lawyers and doctors who have survived juris doctorates and residencies. And soldiers, although my guess is it's a little bit more difficult for them to love their enemies. But there is definitely something unique about the sense of brotherhood bred by competitive sports, linking the body, mind, and soul.

The 18th Man
(New Zealand)

New Zealand was going to be the perfect change of pace. We'd traded the grim poverty of Cambodia for a lush, unspoiled island where sheep outnumber people. The brutal violence of pradal serey for the gentleman's sport of sailing. The New Zealand Board of Tourism was bending over backwards to encourage us to film there, hooking us up with posh parties and the chance to appear in a TV commercial.

But we didn't anticipate the most significant change of all: Team New Zealand, or at least the sailors who manned the boat I was supposed to join, didn't want me there.

Yacht Racing

The idea of using wind to power boats is almost as old as man himself. The ancient Egyptians and Phoenicians began adding cloth sails to their boats over 6,000 years ago. The rest, as they say, is history, full of exploration and discovery, international trade and wars on the sea.

King Charles II of England, exiled to the Netherlands in the 17th century, fell in love with the small Dutch boats called *jaghts*. He brought one back to England, and the idea of sport sailing was born. Soon, "yacht" clubs were springing up all over the world. In 1851, Commodore John Cox Stevens, a member of the New York Yacht Club, sailed a boat called *America* to England in order to challenge the Brits. Cox's boat finished first in a 53-mile race, and he brought an elaborate, cup-shaped silver trophy back to New York. Ever since then, yacht clubs from all over the world have issued challenges and competed for what became known as the "America's Cup."

The boats have evolved over the years, becoming bigger, lighter, and faster, often adding multiple hulls to become catamarans and trimarans. The sport of sailing is evolving as well, as new competitions and numerous debates continue to craft the way races are held.

A legal dispute over the America's Cup led to the creation, in 2009, of the Louis Vuitton Pacific Series, a 10-team, 3-week-long series of 53 races held in Auckland, New Zealand.

The race I was dropping into, the Louis Vuitton Pacific Series, was brand new. But the rivalries that drove it were well established.

Team New Zealand—the crew I was going to join—won the America's Cup in 1995 and 2000. Three years later, the rules of the sport changed to allow clubs to field crews from countries other than their own. A Swiss team called Alinghi took advantage of the opportunity, hiring Team New Zealand's skipper and several of his most important crewmen. Alinghi defeated what was left of New Zealand, taking the America's Cup.

Needless to say, the people of New Zealand weren't very pleased, either with Alinghi or with the traitorous crewmen who had deserted them.

When I arrived in Auckland, Team New Zealand was preparing for payback, having just clinched a spot in the finals against—you guessed it—Alinghi. I was introduced to Winston, one of the "grinders" on the team. Grinders have to be strong; they turn winches to raise and lower the sails as quickly as possible in the heat of a competition where every second counts. But Winston took "strong" to another level. He was a hulk of a guy who made me look small.

I tried to impress him by telling him I knew a little bit about sailing.

"Oh yeah?" he asked. "From where?"

"Club Med," I replied.

Winston smiled and welcomed me to the 17-man crew—as the 18th man.

The 18th man doesn't really have a defined role on the boat, except for one: Stay the hell out of the way of the other 17 guys.

Despite having clinched a spot in the finals, Team New Zealand still had one more preliminary race against the English squad. Nothing serious was on the line, other than pride. I rode in the stern, filming myself with a handheld camera for the show, trying not to interfere with the 17 guys who moved like parts in a machine, raising and lowering sails to take advantage of every subtle shift in the wind.

But there was no way that Team New Zealand was going to let me sail with them during their first race with Alinghi. And when they lost their first race to the Swiss team by 12 seconds, we quickly got the sense that we weren't wanted around there at all.

POSTCARD FROM NEW ZEALAND

I've been to a lot of places, none more beautiful than New Zealand. Imagine the hilly Scottish highlands and Ireland's green pastures with Hawaii's beaches. Nothing poisonous on the entire island. And unspoiled: New Zealand customs won't let as much as a Pop-Tart enter the country.

Not surprisingly, New Zealanders love to be outside. Everybody seems to have an RV that they use to camp up and down the island. But the real draw is the water—they want to be by it, on it, or in it. There are more sailboats per capita than anywhere else in the world. The oceans sustain the people— offering the most incredible seafood I've ever eaten, from snapper to the legendary green-lipped mussels—but it's not just a physical relationship. The water is tied to the country's soul.

My mother read to me from the time I was born, fueling my hopes and dreams.

Above: My first bike. From there on out, I was always going somewhere.

Left: Portrait of the athlete as a young man. Even then, I thought I could take on anybody.

Below: My sister Akila and I in Paris, en route to our first African safari.

Above: Yes, black people can swim. I began competing when I was 6.

Left: My first Michigan game. I knew I was going there—just hadn't filled out the application.

Below: My middle name, Makalani, means "skilled at writing." Here's one of the first books I wrote—and illustrated!

My first uniform at Michigan. No one believed I was a linebacker yet, so they gave me the same number as the kicker.

Not sure what was a bigger thrill: getting drafted by the Giants or seeing my dad wearing my jersey.

Above: I loved Philadelphia, even if the feeling didn't always seem mutual.

Left: Take a picture—it'll last longer (than my time with the Saints).

Below: The Bengals gave me the chance to revive my career.

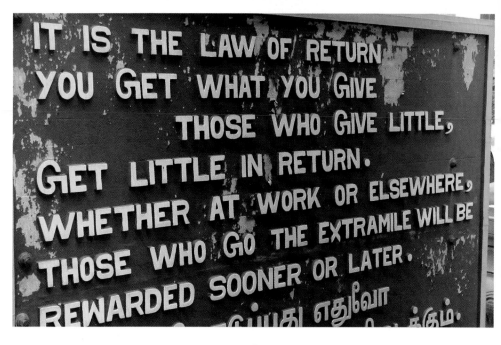

IT IS THE LAW OF RETURN
YOU GET WHAT YOU GIVE
THOSE WHO GIVE LITTLE,
GET LITTLE IN RETURN.
WHETHER AT WORK OR ELSEWHERE,
THOSE WHO GO THE EXTRAMILE WILL BE
REWARDED SOONER OR LATER.

Above: The Hindu temples in Singapore were full of inspirational messages. Here's one I took to heart.

Left: Taking a moment to get my mind right in Switzerland.

Below: My trainer, Tim Adams, had a knack for pushing me to the limit. In Russia, he made me pull him around in a sleigh.

Above: Chilling with my new brothers in Senegal, a place that felt like home from the moment I arrived.

Left: In Italy, getting by (the finish line) with a little help from my friends.

Below: My Croatian water polo team, Gusar Mlini—"the Pirates of Mlini Beach."

Throwing the hammer at the Highland Games in Scotland. Don't you dare call it a skirt!

I have never visited any place more beautiful than New Zealand.

———

When Team New Zealand gave us the stiff arm, we focused on the other stuff that we hoped would make good television. I took sailing lessons from a gruff instructor named Peggy, who made sure I knew the difference between a jib and a jibe. I went to a team party where I met Larry Ellison, the CEO of Oracle and the sponsor of the American crew. Get me around a billionaire, and I get as tongue-tied as any fan.

The most amazing experience might have been bungee jumping off a bridge. *What if something happens? What if this is the time that something goes wrong?* It was the little voice in my head that wants to keep me safe, tucked into bed with a warm glass of milk. But then I heard another voice say, "The hell with it. This is what you want to do." And I jumped, plummeting 12 stories toward the ocean before the rubber band pulled me back.

———

Team New Zealand won a couple of races against Alinghi, and, with a little arm-twisting from the government's tourism bureau, they began to let me back into the fold. Winston showed me how to grind sails, took me heli-fishing on a rocky island, and let me participate in a team workout at the gym. We raced around a buoy in two-man boats, where I did absolutely nothing to convince them that I could actually sail a boat.

After a lot of begging, they finally agreed to let me participate in one of their practices.

One of the most interesting things about sailing is that you are truly at the mercy of the wind. When it blows, it feels like you're flying. When it doesn't, there's nothing you can do but wait.

We spent the first 5 or 6 hours of the practice waiting around for the wind to start blowing. The crewmen were used to this kind of downtime and used it to shoot the proverbial breeze with one another, abiding by one simple rule: On the boat, everyone tells the truth.

You can't lie about anything. If a man asks you if you slept with his girl the night before, and you did, you have to tell him yes. The boat is a place to confide in one another, build honesty and integrity, and develop the kinds of bonds that win races.

We didn't have the history to get into a lot of gossip, but the crew asked me plenty of pointed questions about the things football players do to improve their teams. Not how we got better in the sense of winning or losing, but how we functioned as a unit, the things we did together, the feelings we had toward one another. There wasn't anything subtle about their questions. These guys were really into investigating the essence of a team, tackling the idea with a seriousness I wanted to bring back with me to the Bengals.

Eventually—and suddenly—the wind picked up. For the next hour, I got to grind sails as part of the crew.

Then they dropped me off and replaced me with a real team member so they could practice for another couple of hours.

———

Team New Zealand beat Alinghi to win the Louis Vuitton Cup. I was there to root them on like any other passionate fan. As my friend Zoran Bogdanovic once told me, "People who lose the ability to admire things are inevitably suffering premature death." I admired their teamwork, even if I couldn't be a part of it.

But they let me walk with them to the trophy ceremony, giving me a little taste of what it felt like to be a champion sailor. The next day they agreed to sail an exhibition race against Team New Zealand Two, and I got a chance to wear the uniform and experience the action as a grinder on a real crew.

And when we won the race, my fellow crewmen sprayed me with champagne and tossed me off the dock into the water—a taste of typical rookie hazing.

I may not have set the world on fire with my sailing prowess, but in a lot of ways, I felt like I'd experienced something even richer than the thrill of competition.

GRINDING IT OUT

Grinding. The name says it all, doesn't it? Part cardiovascular exercise, part shoulder and upper-back workout, all pain. Many gyms have grinding machines that provide a great cardiovascular workout that doesn't require the use of your lower body.

But in addition to being a new training modality—one that increased my capacity to do more work, even if it didn't directly apply to football—grinding was a great psychological exercise. Going in a flash from total inactivity to cranking a winch like your life depends on it is a great reminder of your place in the grand scheme of things. It's not always about how much you can lift, how fast you can run, or how hard you can hit—sometimes it's about what you can do to contribute, maximizing your effort as a single part in the service of a whole that is greater than you.

The Travelling Circus

L ike everything else, travelling by plane isn't what it used to be. Some people long for the days when you used to get dressed up to get on a plane. Not me. Everybody was smoking cigarettes. Planes didn't go many places. Couldn't wear my flip-flops.

Other people wish we still lived in a pre-9/11 world, where airport security wasn't such a hassle. No argument here.

But for me, the golden age of travel was just a few years ago: the era of the business-class jet. For just a little more than the price of a normal ticket, you could cross the Atlantic Ocean in style. Carriers like Silverjet, MAXjet, and Eos made you feel like a VIP without charging you like one. I guess it's no surprise they all went out of business.

Nowadays it's all about commercial flights. There's nothing easy about flying. Add a seven-man crew with camera gear, laptops, personal items, and the clothing to cover a 40-day trip to places where temperatures will vary by 80 degrees, and you get a sense of what it was like to travel for the TV show.

A regular travelling circus.

Most of the time, we managed.

Other times, there were experiences like Russia.

One of the dozen or so camera bags we were carrying was missing one of the dozen or so stickers we needed to get through immigration. It took 6 hours of negotiations—plus a handshake and a couple of dollars—before we could see St. Petersburg.

I'm not complaining. That's the price we pay for the ability to travel the world in a way our ancestors could only dream about.

I'll just keep dreaming of the day I have my own jet.

Ice Country
(Russia)

Even if we hadn't already been on the road for over a month, the transition from New Zealand to St. Petersburg, Russia, would have been a shock to the system.

From lush green hills and open water to low grey skies and falling snow.

From T-shirts and shorts to fur caps and overcoats.

From dining on the magical bounty of the sea to pickled everything.

From the 18th man on a 17-man crew to a lone warrior, fighting for survival against master practitioners of the Red Army's official style of combat.

From warm feelings of camaraderie to the creeping sense that everyone, everywhere, was spying on you for the KGB.

SAMBO

The Communist Revolution was a turbulent time. Russia's old ways and traditions were pushed aside, often by force, for what was thought to be new and modern. The very new and modern Soviet Red Army used this strategy to develop a national fighting style.

"Sambo" is actually an acronym: Samozashchita Bez Oruzhiya, or "self-defense without weapons." It was built from the ground up using the best fighting techniques the world had to offer: Japanese judo mixed with traditional Eastern folk wrestling and traditional Western boxing, flavored by everything from Muay Thai to Italian swordsmanship. Nearly every fighting style in the world was evaluated and mined for whatever was most useful toward achieving sambo's primary goals: to disable an opponent as quickly as possible, not with strength, but with speed, decisiveness, and gravity.

Gravity plays a huge role in sambo. The most common sound, at least if you're doing it right, is the thud of your opponent's body hitting the mat. Once he's on the ground, you can force him to submit or otherwise cripple him with a variety of arm and leg holds, focused attacks to the Achilles tendon, or that old standby, squeezing the testicles with great force.

Sambo competitions are very much like any other sport, with the winners and losers determined by judges who award points for various moves and takedowns. But you're never far removed from the mentality that created the sport: Kill or be killed. Every pause or moment of indecision will result in death.

POSTCARD FROM RUSSIA

I know it's a stereotype, but Russia feels like a place full of secrets. There are the paranoid fantasies: That old lady who looks like somebody's grandmother is actually KGB. There are the paranoid realities: Yes, that tall, beautiful woman who keeps checking you out in the bar really is a prostitute. There are the fantastic realities: Step out of the hotel into a below-freezing night, and a woman in a short skirt and heels might ride by on a horse.

The country is full of surprising discoveries. An apartment in a run-down building is a homemade vodka factory. An old warehouse is a martial arts dojo. But the most surprising discovery might be that all of those seemingly stereotypical

ideas about Russian brotherhood are actually true. Behind
cold and secretive exteriors beat warm and open hearts.

One of the first segments we shot in Russia took place at a traditional bathhouse. We sweated it out in a steam room so hot it made me dizzy, then jumped into an ice-bath. Relaxed in a sauna, then took a beating on the back from a leafy tree branch, supposedly to promote circulation.

Russia was full of these sorts of contrasts. Getting through the airport was a bureaucratic nightmare. But a visit to a military base was a trip to the Wild West—if the Wild West were covered in snow and full of sniper rifles to fire, machine guns to spray, and tanks to drive wherever the mood might take you. Nobody was standing in the back saying, "All right, are you ready to fire?" Or, "I'm about to launch an explosive rocket in your direction." Folks were damn casual with their use of mortars. They let me drive a tank!

There wasn't anything casual about Alexander Barakov, the sambo Grandmaster who would be my mentor for the week. Joining his class felt like an initiation into a fraternity. He introduced me to his class with a speech about the seriousness of the training that I was about to embark upon. At the end, he asked me in earnest, "Will you join us?"

"I will join you," I replied.

"Then accept him," he ordered the class, demanding that they hug me.

There were a lot of forced hugs during my time in Russia.

In fact, a lot of the merriment felt forced. It was cold, dark, and damp. Everyone in our crew was exhausted and looking forward to the end of the week, when we'd finally get to go home. When our Russian hosts threw a party in our honor, after a long day of training and filming, the night before another long day of training and filming, none of us wanted to go. Once we were there, no one wanted to stay.

But we had to, lest we offend our hosts, so we kept pace with them as they slammed back drinks, sang patriotic songs, and played festive party games.

I was absolutely miserable, pouting like a child.

I spent my birthday in St. Petersburg, filming a segment with a professional chemist/amateur vodka-maker. We sat for hours in his cramped apartment, eating pickled tomatoes and doing 20 or 30 shots of homemade 80-proof vodka. I mean literally homemade: He was refilling our glasses from the pot he had boiling on his stovetop.

Happy birthday to me.

The sambo practices were 2½ hours long. Coach Alex took his sport and his practices seriously. "You are defending your woman from attacker! Protecting your values!" he'd shout, his version of a motivational speech. Or, "Every stop is a death! Somebody shoot you! Somebody stab you!"

I think it's also safe to say that he had certain preconceptions about the level of dedication he could expect from an American TV personality. Alex wasn't happy the day I decided to drive myself to practice, arriving an hour later than the scheduled start. He was plain furious when I had the audacity, in the middle of practice, to take a sip of water.

"Do you see us take a drink, Da-*hani*?" he yelled. "We don't take a drink during practice!"

I could feel the apeshit switch start to jiggle around. "Do you have any idea what I've been through for the past 30 days?" I wanted to say. "The things I have to do, in addition to this 2½-hour practice, just to keep myself in shape for football? And you're getting on me for taking a damn sip of water?"

But I didn't say any of those things. Instead, I said the two hardest words in the English language: "I'm" and "sorry."

I may not have liked it, but it was his class, his culture, his traditions. I sat down with him the next day for a heart-to-heart, trying to explain where I was coming from, but I did it with as much respect and humility as I could gather.

———————

The day before my big fight, I visited a local fountain where people liked to drop coins for good luck. Only this fountain had a gimmick: If you wanted the fountain's blessing, you had to land the coin on a tiny platform above the water. Otherwise you were just throwing your money away.

I missed on my first try. But on the second, I nailed it. The way I reacted, you'd think I'd won the lottery. That's the funny thing about competition: The size of the achievement doesn't matter; it's achieving it that counts.

An old man standing next to me noticed my celebration. He smiled. He also looked like he could use a little bit of luck—couldn't we all?—so I offered to help him drop one of his own coins onto the platform.

I spent the next half hour holding his wrist, guiding him as he dropped coin after coin onto the platform. Why settle for a little luck when you can have a lot? We hardly understood one another, but we laughed together like kids. Nothing brings people together like competition, except for maybe cooperation.

It was a purely spontaneous moment, one that we never could have scripted. Maybe that's what Russia was all about.

———————

In my final scheduled sambo match, I fought my opponent to a hard-earned draw. It seemed like a particularly apt end to my experience in Russia.

But one of my teammates challenged me to a second match, and, while I'm not saying that he let me win, it felt good to finish as a winner. Alex followed the match with a tearful speech about the progress I'd made, telling me how proud he was to have coached me.

I may have been heading back to the States physically, mentally, and spiritually drained, but with a newfound respect for the kinds of unexpected relationships that enrich our lives.

WORKING WITH WHAT YOU'VE GOT

Russia was the last trip I took with Tim, who got a full-time job with the L.A. Kings. But he wasn't about to get sentimental. Although the sambo practices were exhausting, they weren't grueling enough to satisfy Tim. He decided to surprise me one afternoon with a workout he'd designed specifically for Russia.

Actually, he hadn't designed it as much as stolen it from *Rocky IV.*

We drove for an hour into the snowy countryside. When we got out of the van, Tim handed me an ax. "Start chopping," he said, pointing to a fallen log.

After an hour of pulverizing wood, Tim led me to a horse-driven sleigh. Without a horse. He handed me the harness.

I put on the harness and dragged Tim through the woods.

When he finally released me, we jogged through the snow until we reached a barn where, just like in the movie, a second harness hung from the ceiling. I used it to do pullups until my muscles damn near exploded.

You don't need a gym to experience a total-body workout that will leave you sore for days. You can almost always work with whatever you've got.

Cincinnati, Part One

O n a scale of 1 to 10, Cincinnati is a solid 7.5.

Downtown Cincinnati, which sits right on the Ohio River, is in the middle of a successful urban revival. The commercial district is surrounded by rolling hills and lots of trees.

There's a great deal of history here. Cincinnati was the final stop on the Underground Railroad, literally representing freedom to escaped slaves.

It's an incredibly polite city. You'll hear a lot of "How can I help you's" from people who really mean it.

Yes, there's a lot to recommend about Cincinnati, as long as you're not expecting a 9 or a 10.

When I first got here, people would tell me about this or that great restaurant I *had* to try. I'd get excited, go in expecting some sort of gourmet miracle—and wind up disappointed.

On the other hand, there have been plenty of places people told me were good. I've visited them with moderate expectations, and, more times than not, I've been pleasantly surprised.

Cincinnati is the place where I can slow down, take stock of my life and the direction it's heading without feeling the need to be hip-deep in the next-next thing. It's a place where I can get everything I need while eliminating the phrase "What do you mean you don't have that?" from my vocabulary. I can restore my focus, resimplify my life.

So nice.

Back to Africa
(Senegal)

I spent the next 2 months in Cincinnati, mostly working out with the team. Despite the previous season's troubles, our goal was the same as it ever was: the Super Bowl. But it was relaxing to spend a few weeks in the same place, especially because of what was ahead: *Dhani Tackles the Globe* was picked up for a second season. That meant five new episodes before training camp, at least 4 months of football, then five more episodes of the show.

I had to be in Cincinnati for the Bengals' minicamp in June, so Senegal would have to be a stand-alone episode. I didn't have any idea it would turn out to be such a stand-alone place.

POSTCARD FROM SENEGAL

I hate to say it, but when you think about "Africa," you're probably thinking about Senegal.

North Africa is way too modern to get lumped in with the rest of the continent, at least in the eyes of North Africans. A lot of South Africa isn't that much different from Europe. But Senegal, the westernmost tip of West Africa, still feels like Africa. There are aspects that are modern, but you're never very far removed from the past. Bush country is much more prevalent than urban development. Just a few miles off a four-lane superhighway, you'll stumble across an old-world village straight out of National Geographic. People still visit witch doctors and sing songs to honor their ancestors.

Yes, Senegal is Africa, with all of its glory and all of its issues. And while I don't want to get all caught up in some kind of "back to my roots" thing, there's a part of me that feels like I'm finally home.

I knew I was in Africa before I got off the plane in Dakar.

I don't know how I knew; I just *knew*. There was something different about the air. A different feeling inside of me.

Part of that feeling was very easy to explain: I was surrounded by people who looked like me.

Potomac, Maryland, where I grew up, is less than 4 percent black. At the University of Michigan, that number might have doubled. I'm not saying I grew up feeling like part of an oppressed minority, but facts are facts: I've spent my entire life living among people who look different than me. It's always been my "normal."

Travelling the world usually intensifies those differences. Sure, England had a few African blokes. Singapore has a decent Malaysian population. But most of the time I was the oddity, the outlier, the not-so-proverbial black swan.

Now I was in Senegal, where "ethnic differences" referred to what tribe you were from, not the color of your skin. I was in the cradle of everything, getting wrapped up in a loincloth—one that looked and felt an awful lot like a diaper—by "Bombardier," a Senegalese wrestler whose enormous size made me look like a baby.

I was home.

LUTTE WRESTLING

Every culture has some form of wrestling, each with its own techniques and technicalities. Mastering the subtle differences is often the difference between success and failure: You have to know the right moves if you want to anticipate your opponent's next move, dominate him with one of your own, and impress the judges along the way.

"Lutte" is French for "struggle," the name the French colonialists applied to the wrestling they observed among the natives. And at its essence, that's what Senegal's national sport is: a primal struggle between two men.

You don't win with fancy moves and reversals, or points from a judge; you win by defeating your opponent. Knock him out of the ring, you win. Make him sit on the ground, you win. Get his head to touch the ground, you win. Put him on his hands and knees, you win. Force him to lie on his belly, you win—while humiliating him in the worst way possible.

Lutte wrestling was the way a Senegalese man proved his manhood, whether to attract a wife or to bring pride to his family and village. Not much has changed—the sport's champions are revered by the people, still inspiring poets called griots to write and sing songs celebrating their achievements.

The sport is not without some technique. Fights may be held *avec frappe* (with punches) or *sans frappe* (without punches). But the keys to success lie in physical training, power of spirit, and strength of heart.

Physical conditioning isn't just part of a lutte wrestler's life—it *is* his life. The entire country is like a 24-hour gym. Go almost anywhere in Dakar and you'll be surrounded by people doing pushups, running in the sand, or working out with whatever heavy objects happen to be at hand, from an automotive chassis to concrete blocks.

Almost as much effort is spent on spiritual fitness. Lutte wrestlers tend to be extremely superstitious, whether it comes to washing their clothes (many don't), applying mysterious lotions, or rubbing their bodies with sacred rocks. It's common practice to visit witch doctors the day before a fight. The prefight ritual usually includes a *sim* ceremony— short for *simba*—in which wrestlers dress up as lions and perform an ancient dance to channel their spiritual energy.

As for heart, that's just built into the culture. The Senegalese were, historically, the people most likely to revolt on slave ships. You don't have to spend much time with them to understand why.

———

The country's national symbol is the baobab tree. Understand the baobab, and you'll start to understand Senegal.

Many of these trees live for hundreds of years, nearing 100 feet in height and 50 feet in circumference. Their hollows are used to store water. The largest trees may store human remains: Famous griots—the storytellers who chronicle Senegal's history through their poetry and song—are often entombed within the trees, which continue to grow around them, literally intertwining man and nature.

Nearly every part of the tree has an important purpose or application. The fruit, often called "monkey bread," is either mashed into porridge or pulped into a juice that has six times as much vitamin C as oranges and twice the calcium of milk.

It's also reputed to work as well as Viagra.

The baobab's seeds can be grilled and eaten or used to make soap. The leaves are either dried and ground into powder—used as everything from an anti-inflammatory to a diarrhea remedy—or pounded into a gruel loaded with protein, calcium, and iron. The bark is believed to fight fever and improve digestion.

Every lutte wrestler is expected to adopt a name. My coach, the 6-foot-7, 300-pound Bombardier, certainly lived up to his, reigning as lutte's undisputed champion for many years. I settled on "Gwiggy-bond," combining a nickname for the baobab tree with the last name of my favorite action hero.

Bombardier didn't speak much English, and I understood even less Wolof (his native tongue), so we needed a translator. But we started communicating the moment we met, staring one another down in the universal way that one competitor sizes up another. It's pretty amazing when you think about it—without any verbal communication, using only our eyes, we were able to establish ourselves to one another, forging the beginnings of what would grow into a deep bond.

Most of our training revolved around physical fitness. We did duck-walks through the sand. Concrete blocks became pushup bars. A piece of rebar with a wheel from a car on each side worked as well as any bench-press bar.

We worked on technique, Bombardier teaching me the best ways to drive an opponent into the ground. I enjoyed spending time with him and the other wrestlers, who seemed to talk as much as I did. I asked my translator to tell me what they were saying.

"They're telling one another that they're too fat. Too skinny. Not strong enough."

Trash-talk is also universal.

We also spent time on a few activities that didn't make sense to me, at least not immediately. Bombardier told me about the griots, he showed me how to dress up like a lion and perform the sim dance (supposedly channeling the animal's spirit), and the day before my match, he took me to see a witch doctor.

We had spent most of our time in Dakar, Senegal's relatively modern capital, and left the city on a four-lane highway that could have existed in any modern country. But when we got off the road and drove for about 20 minutes into the desert, the car might just as well have been a time machine. We came to a stop in an African village, where we were greeted by a village elder who had a look in his eyes that commanded respect.

The witch doctor.

Senegal is technically an Islamic country—Amadou, my translator, had plenty to say about our driver Bomba, who he considered to be "a sloppy Muslim." Islamic law doesn't have much tolerance for witch doctors or any other kind of pagan mystics. Just don't try to explain that to the many Senegalese who believe that these holy men have greater powers than their regular medical doctors.

Given an infant mortality rate pushing 1 in 10, they might not be wrong.

I believe in science, especially medical science. But I also believe that some people exist on different spiritual planes than I do. I don't think there's any way to explain it, at least not in scientific terms, but it's definitely something that I have felt at certain times in my life.

This visit to the witch doctor was one of those times. His ancient ritual left me feeling quiet, serene, at peace.

Had he bestowed me, as many lutte wrestlers believe, with invincibility?

Who knows?

All I do know is that the mind is a powerful weapon, and after a week in Senegal, my mind was feeling right.

In America, sports are all about the modern.

We pay homage to many of our old traditions. Baseball purists, for example, might tell you that the game looks the same as it always did— but it's just not true.

Today's professional athletes compete in enormous stadiums with piped-in music and high-definition scoreboards. They wear uniforms constructed from advanced microfibers, state-of-the-art helmets, masks, cleats, and gloves. Rules are constantly added, updated, or thrown out completely. Instant replay is used to settle disputes.

We place an enormous emphasis on breaking records. It's not about honoring the past as much as outpacing it.

Lutte wrestling, on the other hand, takes a completely opposite approach to the idea of sport. Not only does it look the same as it always has, but everything about it seems intent on bringing the past into the present.

The matches don't take place in a grand arena; any sandy surface will do. Ours was a blocked-off area of the street.

Don't let this fool you into believing that there's an amateurish or low-rent feel to the sport. As Bombardier and I walked down the street, we were followed by hundreds of fans dancing with frenzied passion. Despite the fact that he'd been retired for several years, dozens of people wore T-shirts with his picture on them. Several women broke into hysterical crying at the sight of him.

We were accompanied by the griots, who sang songs about Bombardier—his greatest fights, but also his parents, his grandparents, and their parents and grandparents, thus establishing him as not just an individual but the latest incarnation of a long and proud tradition.

When we finally reached the ring, all the fighters—including me—performed the sim dance, flexing for the crowd, channeling the strength and courage of the lion. In the NFL, we'll often do dances to celebrate our unique greatness. The sim dance was about honoring the forces that made us that way.

All the lead-up suddenly made sense. We weren't wrestling to break records, to outdo the ancestors. We were fighting to honor them, to compete in the same way that they had, to thank them for showing us how to get there. We were showing our gratitude to the mysterious spirit that allowed us to compete.

None of the matches lasted more than a few minutes. Many were over in a few seconds. Whether I was inspired by my surroundings, lent invincibility by my visit to the witch doctor, or the beneficiary of a career mostly defined by knocking other large men off their feet, I was able to put my opponent on the ground.

The crowd began to chant: "Gwiggybond . . . Gwiggybond . . . Gwiggybond!" Somebody hoisted me onto his shoulders. It was both a final reminder and the perfect metaphor for my experience in Senegal.

We're all riding on the shoulders of the people who came before us, benefitting from a power and a spirit that is much larger than we are.

GETTING YOUR MIND RIGHT

So much about sports is psychological. I don't use witch doctors or ancient dances, but I do have a ritual that helps put me into the frame of mind I need to compete at a high level on a weekly basis.

Two hours before a game starts, I'll get my crew socks from the equipment manager. I cut off the tops. I don't know why I cut my socks, except that it makes me feel more comfortable to do it. When you find a uniform that you feel comfortable in, you've found a uniform that allows you to make the most plays on the field.

Then I take a shower. I can't just choose any shower—I have to count the showerheads until I find the right number. Seven from one side and eight from the other. If that one is occupied, then I'll take the one that is three from one side and 11 from the other side. I know that this habit makes me sound like Jack Nicholson in *As Good As It Gets*. Yes, every-body makes fun of me. But, like everything else, it helps me to get my mind right.

I hang out for a while in the shower, stretching. Some people use the whirlpool. I like being in the shower. The whirlpool is for relaxing. The shower invigorates me.

When I get out of the shower, I go to the training room, where I tell Dan—the only guy I want taping my ankles—to save a spot for me. I visit my locker to put my pants and shirt on, then back to the training room so Dan can tape me up. Back to my locker, where I put on my right sock, left sock, right half-sock, left half-sock, right sleeve, left sleeve, and, finally, right shoe, left shoe.

Then I head out to the field.

I always work out on the same sideline as the tunnel. I walk to the goal line, run to the 50-yard line, and run back to the goal.

Then I skip from the goal line to the 30 and skip back. Front lunges to the 30 and back. Side lunges to the 15, switch directions, and continue to the 30. Swinging kicks, channeling my inner Rockette, as I move back to the goal.

After some core exercises in the middle of the field, I run back into the locker room. I never sign autographs, take pictures, or talk to anybody while I'm outside. I just shut them out. It's nothing personal—I'm just getting my mind right.

Inside the locker room, I'll get my Toradol shot. Same spot in my shoulder every time—I'm thinking about getting a little dot tattooed there to honor the process. I tape up my thumbs. Five minutes before the linebackers are scheduled to go out, I put on my pads and gloves, and make sure my helmet is properly adjusted. Then I go work out with the team, usually a seven-on-seven drill.

Some rituals are individual, some are done in groups. The defense brings it up, asserting our togetherness, then we run back inside.

I go directly to the training room, where I get my wrists taped. Sometimes I'll cut my fingernails. But if I cut one fingernail, I'll cut all my fingernails, because that's what I did the night I caused a fumble and made three tackles in just nine plays.

I never cut my toenails. Chad Ochocinco says you're never supposed to cut your toenails before a game. You will play terribly if you cut your toenails. Who am I to argue?

Finally, I'm ready to hit the field.

You can laugh at the ritual—plenty of people do—but I believe it puts me in a positive place. I can make better decisions, play with higher production, and experience a lot more good fortune.

Find your ritual. Use it to make your mind right.

A NOTE FROM JONATHAN FIERRO, PRODUCER

We're leaving Senegal, and it's taking forever to go through customs. We finally get through and all the bags are in, when we have to go through "secondary security." One of the security guys comes up to me and says, "We need to take you down below. There's some stuff that looks a little shaky in your bags."

I'm like, Wow, do I go with this guy, do I not go with this guy? *So I say to Dhani, "Do not let this plane leave. I don't care what you have to do, do not let this plane leave."*

So they take me below and start pulling out my gear. I think one of our batteries is beeping. It takes me a half hour to convince them that it's just a battery.

Finally, they let me go. I cross the tarmac, walk up the stairs, and there is Dhani, at the doorway, with his foot in the door. He's not letting that plane go anywhere without me.

That kind of tells you what his thinking is. Loyalty. Fuck, the guy's the host of the show. He didn't have to do that. But it was nice to see that he did.

Give Yourself Some (Extra) Credit

People don't give themselves enough credit.

"I'm not smart enough."

"I'm not fast enough."

"I'm not strong enough."

"It hurts too much."

There's always an "I'm not enough" or "It's too much." And a lot of the time, it's bullshit.

It's easy to underestimate true potential and true ability. Studies show that you only use something like 3 percent of your brain. So what's going on with the other 97 percent? A 100-pound woman can lift a car if her child is in need. How come we can't access that strength any other time? Linguists say you can learn 20 languages by the time you're 7 years old. Yet most people know only one language.

There is a wall, some sort of impasse inside of us. We suspect that the potential is there, but for whatever reason, most of the time we're not able to push through it. Why else are there so many self-help books on the bestseller list?

Maybe you don't need a book. Maybe it's just saying to yourself, "I have an incredible amount of potential and I am going to utilize every damn bit of it and I don't care what anybody says."

Dream.

Work.

Work some more.

Watch it become reality.

No Problem for Jón Páll
(Iceland)

During the summer, the sun doesn't set—it sits, lighting Iceland for 23 hours each day.

The landscape is literally so otherworldly that NASA used it to train astronauts for their landing on the moon. Enormous glaciers cover a 10th of the country. Miniature horses run wild. The rugged mountains are home to Europe's most powerful waterfall. Volcanoes are an everyday part of life, creating spectacular geysers, natural lagoons with honest-to-God healing powers, and sulfuric soil warm enough to cook in.

What better place on earth to redefine my perception of what is possible?

POSTCARD FROM ICELAND

The Vikings spread throughout Scandinavia, but nowhere is their influence more alive than in Iceland. The people treasure strength, aggressiveness, and an indomitable spirit as their birthright.

The country itself is full of natural wonders. The nearly endless summer sunlight creates massive amounts of plankton, triggering an explosion at the bottom of the food chain that leads to some of the richest fishing waters in the world. A natural saltwater blue lagoon contains enough minerals in its silt to give it medicinal powers. Volcanic soil, with temperatures reaching 200 degrees, has helped Icelanders cook and pre-serve food since the Viking days.

But the people don't take any of it for granted. When an Ice-lander kills a sheep, he eats the whole sheep, including the entire head. (The eyes are considered quite the delicacy.) The con-struction of a proposed hydroelectric plant at the base of Europe's most powerful waterfall was halted when a single woman, unwilling to live with the desecration of the natural beauty, threatened to hurl herself over the side.

The entire country rallied around her. What could be more Icelandic than knowing what you have and being willing to die to protect it?

STRONGMAN COMPETITION

Despite the Viking heritage, the people of Iceland have a democratic bent, including a parliamentary system over 1,000 years old. But when it came to divvying up the daily catch from the sea, Iceland's fisher-men used pure meritocracy: The strongest man got the most fish.

The fishermen would establish the pecking order before setting out each morning by power-lifting a series of rocks, the heaviest being well over 300 pounds. The guy who lifted the biggest rocks got the big-gest share of the catch.

What started as necessity ultimately became recreation. When Icelanders would gather for festivals, they challenged one another to various feats of strength: lifting or throwing heavy rocks, racing with large sacks of feed, walking as far as they could with a 200-pound weight in each hand. Over the years (and thanks to a demand in the 1970s for televised "World's Strongest Man" competitions), the activi-ties have evolved into a more structured sport.

Early in my strongman training, my coach, Hjalti, took me to a cemetery, where we paid tribute to one of Iceland's most famous strongmen, Jón Páll Sigmarsson.

Jón Páll, the Babe Ruth of strongman competitions—he was crowned World's Strongest Man four times during the 1980s—is considered a national hero. He's remembered most for two things, aside from his massive strength.

The first was his can-do spirit. The saying "No problem for Jón Páll" is the Icelandic equivalent of "Just do it."

The second was his infamous quote: "There is no point in being alive if you can't do deadlift," referring to his ability to lift enormous weights off the ground. Jón Páll was only 32 when he died of a heart attack brought on by—you guessed it—a deadlift.

Ironic? On several levels. But it helped me to get a feel for Iceland's tremendous sense of national pride. The competitors I met weren't just lifting rocks—they believed that they were waging war against their human limitations, and that failure meant death.

The first place Hjalti took me was a gym where I attempted to lift a 200-pound weight above my head.

I did it. Couldn't have been prouder of myself.

Five minutes later, I watched a woman perform the same lift. Damn. The Icelandic people were tough.

The next test came near the ocean, where Hjalti showed me the rocks that fishermen once used to determine who was going to get the largest share of the daily catch. I lifted the 50-pound rock, no problem. Struggled with the 220-pound rock, but I got it up. But the final rock, the 340-pounder?

"I can't do that one," I admitted, after giving it my best.

Fewer fish for me.

We moved from the training into our increasingly normal routine of exploring the country's landmarks and culture. The film crew was in heaven thanks to the summer's 23-hour days. We were used to racing against sundown to grab a shot; now we could lose track of time and laugh when we looked at our watches to see that it was 1:30 in the morning.

I tried my hand at fishing. Cooked a meal in volcanic soil. Visited a geyser. Swam in a natural blue lagoon. Ate an entire sheep's head. But the bulk of what I had to do was bulk up.

Hjalti took me to a farm, where I practiced racing back and forth with 80-pound sacks of feed, tossing them into the back of a truck. He also had me use a rope to pull him as he sat on the back of an ATV. Hjalti is not a small man. Their combined weight was over 1,200 pounds. But I managed.

Had to.

In the competition, I'd be pulling an SUV.

When it comes to lifting rocks, there's no heavier test than the Husafell Stone, a triangular stone that weighs about 385 pounds. Fortunately, the shape makes it a little easier than you'd think to lift it. Not easy, mind you, just easier.

Which is why strongman competitors don't just lift the Husafell Stone—the contest is to see who can walk the farthest with it.

"Baby steps," I kept telling myself as I struggled with the giant rock.

But the most daunting trial is the Atlas Stone. These rocks weigh *only* 200 to 300 pounds, and you *only* have to lift them onto an elevated platform. It's called an Atlas Stone, however, because of its resemblance to a globe: They are almost perfect spheres. Without any handhold to get a grip, they are nearly impossible to lift.

Or so it seemed the first time I tried. "I can't," I said. "It's too heavy."

"It's all about the spirit," Hjalti assured me. "The Viking spirit. Try again."

So I did, telling myself it wasn't a 250-pound rock, but a helium balloon. "It's a balloon!" I yelled, as I managed to lift it up and over a 4-foot bar.

"It's like a war," said Boris, a trainer who was helping me with my technique. "If you give up, you lose."

Soon I was lifting progressively heavier Atlas Stones like it was my job.

"I'm almost proud of you," Hjalti said.

A NOTE FROM TIM ADAMS, TRAINER

There is a cost to everything Dhani does. One of the times he lifted an Atlas Stone, he tweaked his back a little bit. So we had to do some therapy.

Would I have preferred him not to tweak his back? Absolutely. But was it good for him to prove to himself and everybody else that, yeah, he can lift this stone up and do whatever anybody else does? I think that was good, too.

The strongman competition involved about a dozen competitors and five events. I removed the words "I can't" from my vocabulary and went to work.

I pulled an SUV, from a seated position, with a tow rope.

I ran with an enormous rock in one direction, dropped it, then carried five 80-pound sacks back the other way, tossing them into the back of a truck. Scored the fastest time in the group.

I performed an overhead lift that wasn't just a test of strength, but also one of endurance—I wasn't allowed to drop it until the referee blew a whistle.

I carried the famed 385-pound Husafell Stone, hoping to make it 100 feet. I went 130.

Finally, there were the Atlas Stones. I was last to go, so I'd already seen every other competitor fail to lift the last stone.

Not me. I tossed that rock up and into an elevated barrel.

When the dust settled, I finished the competition in second place. In the process, I had completely redefined my understanding of my strength, unlocking power I didn't know I had.

Maybe there was a little Viking spirit in me after all.

THE ATLAS STONE

The spherical Atlas Stone is far from the heaviest weight you can lift—they usually don't weigh more than 275 pounds. It's the shape, or more accurately, the weight distribution, that makes the stone so difficult to lift.

When you lie on your back and lift a bar, the weight is distributed in a way that allows you to use your center of mass—the most powerful part of your body—to elevate the weight. The spherical Atlas Stone forces you to rely on strength outside your center of mass.

It seems impossible at first. You can't grab it. You can't hold it. You have to cradle it, reaching around the stone and clasping your hands, pulling yourself into a squatting position. Setting it on your lap, you have to readjust your arms to cup the stone. Then it's a matter of directing power through your hips to thrust the rock up and onto a platform.

It's heavy as shit. But that's the point. Lifting weights that seem impossible not only benefits your body, improving its maximum capacity—it also breaks through the barriers in your mind, allowing you to prove to yourself that you can do almost anything.

A Selfless,
Self-Centered Egotist

People sometimes think that I'm egotistical, self-centered, or hardheaded.

I believe that I do most of what I do in order to help others. Granted, I might be better because of it, but I'm trying to lay a pathway for those who may not have the same opportunities I've had.

Okay, maybe that sounds a little egotistical, self-centered, or hardheaded. And maybe sometimes I am. But in my heart, I'm a selfless guy with a genuine concern for everybody around me. I do things for the future. I do things for my friends, my family, my children (whenever I might have them), and the legacy I am leaving.

This belief allows me to take things head-on. If I get hit on the head and fall down, I have to get myself back up, because others are counting on me.

Mike Zimmer, the Bengals' defensive coordinator, likes to say, "Who's going to do it? You want Joe to do it? You want Bobby to do it?"

To hell with that. You do it. If you don't set the example, if you don't set the priority for yourself, then what are you going to do? You're just a sheep.

I'm not a sheep. I'm a wolf, and I don't have any interest in the back of the pack.

My dad used to call me "Lone Wolf." But just because I'm trying to get to the head of the pack doesn't mean I'm alone. I know there's a pack behind me, pushing me forward.

Tre Amici
(Italy)

When Americans talk about home ownership, you'll often hear terms like "flipping a property" or "trading up." The idea is to buy something, maybe improve it a little, then get rid of it, making enough money to move into something that is, supposedly, bigger and better.

One of the first things I noticed about Italy is the way people deal with their homes. A lot of grown kids live at home with their mother and father, even after they've started their own families. They just build a house on top of the house on top of the house on top of the house, creating the space they need. Even after generations, the family is living in the same house. Nobody's talking about "flipping" —they're looking at the house they have and figuring out how to make it best suit their family's needs.

POSTCARD FROM ITALY

The term "la dolce vita" is often used to describe the Italian mentality, but until you get there, it's hard to grasp its meaning.

For me, la dolce vita meant a family dinner that went on for hours, with fresh pasta handmade by a real Italian mama with eggs from her henhouse, in a ragú created from the ingredients she'd grown in her garden. And drinking Bassano del Grappa's namesake spirit, still produced using the same careful techniques that have been used for generations. And

riding a bike, experiencing the open air and the singular beauty of an old and scenic country.

IL GRAN FONDO DEL MONTE GRAPPA

The origins of the bicycle are shrouded in legend. Some believe that it was designed by a disciple of Leonardo da Vinci. Others point to the year 1816, when severe climate activity throughout Europe destroyed much of the crops, causing many horses to die and a clever German inventor to develop an alternative. Whatever its origins, the bicycle captured the European imagination, spreading throughout the continent, each country making alterations and improvements on the original design.

It didn't take long for the Europeans to start competing with one another to see who could ride faster. The first organized race, a 1200-meter sprint, was held in Paris in 1868. A year later, an international group of riders raced 76 miles from Paris to Rouen, walking their bikes up the more difficult stretches. Today, the three Grand Tours—the Tour de France, Giro d'Italia, and Vuelta a España—each covering over 2,000 miles, are among the most popular sporting events in all of Europe.

But they're not the only races. On any given weekend in Italy, some village is probably holding a *gran fondo,* literally "a large distance or depth." The Gran Fondo del Monte Grappa has both, covering 80 miles, the first quarter or so a grueling climb up a 10 percent grade to the top of an 1,800-foot peak.

Bikes have always been a huge part of my life. When I was younger, I used to ride my BMX everywhere. I went to a place called "the Alligator

Pit" with my friends—we skidded through mud and used the hills to jump over just about everything. There was also a dirt track near where I lived. We'd race there for hours.

My bike never felt like just a toy to me. It was my primary form of transportation before I had a car. My parents never held me back from going wherever I was able to go, as long as I could get back. The bike was my key to the world, the freedom to be able to take off.

So I was excited to get to Italy, where bikes weren't hobby, but passion. My plan was to avoid cars altogether, biking everywhere we needed to go.

But I had never been in a bike race. And I knew I wasn't going to win the Gran Fondo del Monte Grappa.

Every other sport I'd tried for the show—hell, every other sport I'd tried in my life—I thought I could win. Maybe I didn't have a great chance, but if things broke the right way . . .

One look at the intense mountain climb that was the beginning of Monte Grappa, and I knew there was no way.

Champion cyclists train every day at their craft. Champion cyclists don't weigh 235 pounds. There wasn't any amount of positive belief in the world that would allow me to win an 80-mile bike race against 800 well-trained and much lighter racers. I wasn't even sure I was going to be able to finish.

The "I can't finish" mind-set, however, was one that I could challenge. My first step was finding someone who had done it before.

I found that person in Cristiano Citton, a native of Bassano del Grappa. Not only had Cristiano spent his life riding these mountains, but he'd also represented Italy twice in the Olympics. He took me on rides every day, teaching me what it was going to take to complete the course.

But Cristiano wasn't my only role model—everywhere I went, I met someone who had blazed a trail before me.

I visited Battaglin Cicli, where Giovanni Battaglin helped fit me for the Bentley of custom-made bicycles: $8,000 for 13 pounds of composite metal. Battaglin wasn't only a bike-maker, however, but a bike champion: In 1981, he won the Giro d'Italia and the Vuelta a España.

For my racing jersey, I went to see Marcel Tinazzi, who created a custom outfit for me. Before he became one of Europe's most renowned makers of bicycle clothing, he was a championship racer in his own right, cycling professionally with a French team in the 1970s and '80s.

Everywhere I went, I found someone who had done it before me. And it wasn't just limited to cycling.

I met Antonio Nardini, who showed me how his family made grappa, a 100-proof spirit made from grapes, using basically the same process that they'd come up with in the 18th century.

Cristiano invited me to his home for dinner, where his mother showed me how to make pasta using the same techniques she'd learned from her grandmother.

I started to believe that I could complete this ride because other people had done it before me.

As I thought about that, it dawned on me that I'd also be showing other people that it could be done. There weren't going to be any other football players riding in this race. Hell, there weren't any other black people in this race. Just because I wasn't going to be the winner didn't mean I couldn't blaze a new trail.

A NOTE FROM COMMANDER SAMUEL L. JONES

There are certain things that I wanted Dhani to understand about himself and for him to be able to rest in as he would go through this life.

I have to be of character that will let him see what it is possible to do. So the kinds of things I've always done in my life have been a legacy that he could look at and study if he ever needed to. For example, he could read news articles about me at the University of Michigan and learn about the kinds of things I got involved in, so that he always knew what kind of person I was. Blazing a trail, if you will.

The first 3 hours of the race took us straight up a 10 percent grade. In practical terms, every mile was the equivalent of riding up a 50-story building. For nearly 20 damn miles.

A lot of the training I'd done with Cristiano was alongside other beginners. None of us were expected to survive those first 3 hours without stopping for a break, catching some wind, or getting off the bike to push it up the hill for a while.

I decided that I was going to pedal up that hill, without stopping, no matter what. I had to develop a new kind of mental fortitude, a series of tricks and tales to keep my legs pumping and my brain—which was begging me to quit—occupied with other ideas.

I told myself that yes, this was going to be one of those days, but that I would survive. Anyone who doubted me could go home now.

I told myself that what does not kill me makes me stronger, and this wasn't going to kill me.

I asked myself how many other black men had biked this race, and promised myself that I was going to be the guy to do it. I was going to be that name in the history books. You may not have heard of him, but look him up. He's a bad motherfucker.

Without these mantras, I couldn't have made it. But the mantras weren't enough.

Cristiano probably could have ridden this race facing backwards and finished in the top 10. Instead, he hung back from the crowd and rode with me, pushing me on.

I wasn't wearing the jersey that Marcel had designed for me—the crew found me a sponsor instead—but that didn't seem to bother Marcel, who joined us on the ride.

As we neared the top of the hill, there was Cristiano's mama, a woman I'd just met, cheering me on like she'd known me my whole life.

The desire to blaze your own trail might get you up in the morning. But there's no more powerful force than the support of friends, family, teammates, and whoever else is important in your life to help you get to where you need to go.

The winner of the Gran Fondo del Monte Grappa did it in 3 hours.

It took us almost 7. But I made it all the way up that hill without stopping.

I wouldn't have finished without my new brothers, Cristiano and Marcel. Watching them do it with me reminded me that I could.

I recently got a tweet from the guys at Battaglin who built my bike: "You have family in Italy! Come visit us any time! Come riding with us!"

There's no better feeling than winning, and it's great to be the lone wolf at the head of the pack. But sometimes it's enough to know that you have a pack to support you.

CYCLING

I love my car. It's fun to drive fast. It gets me where I need to go.

But why drive, I always remind myself, when you can ride?

Cycling is great exercise. A perfect form of active recovery. It's good for the environment and doesn't cost you gas money. It puts you in touch with a sense of freedom, knowing that you can get where you need to go using your own power.

I ride my bike everywhere in Cincinnati. You may need to shift your mind-set a little bit (and buy a warm hat), but you'll be happy you did.

Modes of Expression

A NOTE FROM DR. NANCY JONES

Dhani needs structure. He likes structure, to some degree. But he needs structure and flexibility. He can't have 100 percent structure.

I think that's true of everybody. But people who are creative, they have to have that flexibility in their life.

I n college I had the opportunity to experiment with many types of art. I wrote poetry, performed in videos with my friends, painted, and took my camera everywhere. I started taking pictures of myself; I'd mount them on frames I'd created and add painted imagery over the top, my own twist on something I'd seen in a movie. As I got better, I used the technique in an attempt to capture the essence of other people, as well. The project became a huge part of the major that I created: self-representation.

Once I got to the pros, my focus had to narrow. But I still look for opportunities to flex my creative muscles whenever I can, whether it's writing poetry (often on my BlackBerry) or standing in as a guest conductor for the Philadelphia Pops.

I design my own bow ties, many of which I donate to charity—I have a foundation called Bow Ties for a Cause. We recently sold nearly

250 ties at a fund-raiser for the Juvenile Diabetes Research Foundation, taking in around $15,000 for the organization. I do a lot of work with Lance Armstrong's Livestrong Foundation, and, in tribute to my friend Kunta, support many groups fighting leukemia and lymphoma.

I bring my camera on all my trips; it's a Canon Mark II 5d. I've gotten a little better since college. Maybe a lot better. A gallery in Cincinnati recently hosted an exhibition of the photos I took on my trip to Senegal.

I am the cofounder of a creative agency, VMG ("Velocity Made Good") Creative. Despite how this may sound, it's not just a vanity project: Our clients include Ralph Lauren, and Procter & Gamble.

The wall next to my bed is a giant chalkboard. I use it to write down my new ideas whenever they strike me. It's a crazy-ass board that doesn't make sense to anybody except me.

Which is exactly what I'm trying to say.

I don't create art to puff myself up, even though I'm proud of my work. We all have an artistic side that we have to express if we want to live a life that feels whole.

City of Artists
(Croatia)

When people think of Croatia, the first thing that comes to mind is often war. Just 20 years ago, the country was fighting for its independence. The city of Dubrovnik, an old and beautiful city often called "the Pearl of the Adriatic," was bombarded by artillery for 7 months, killing over a hundred people and damaging or destroying much of the city's historic architecture.

But Dubrovnik isn't a city of warriors—it's a city of poets, actors, and musicians. Every summer, a 45-night arts festival gets kicked off by a symbolic gesture: The mayor hands the city keys to the artists, reminding them that the city belongs to them.

In fact, Dubrovnik made the decision to completely demilitarize itself in the 1970s, hoping to put an end to war altogether. While the strategy may have failed, the city survived, rebuilt itself, and is thriving today.

Dubrovnik is the birthplace of many of Croatia's most famous artists, poets, playwrights, comedians, and singers. When it comes to sports, however, the people turn their attention toward an artistry of a different sort: competitive water polo.

WATER POLO

As the rugby craze swept England during the 19th century, it was only natural that someone tried to play the game in the water. "Water rugby" demonstrations were soon being held throughout the country, displays of strength and swimming skill that were as bruising as the sports they were based on.

In 1877, a Scottish swimming expert named William Wilson wrote the first official set of rules for the game, which he played with a soft rubber ball called a *pulu*. The game quickly grew into water polo, which was popular enough to appear at the 1900 Olympic Games. Today it's the longest-running team sport in Olympic history.

Over time, the rules evolved, eliminating a lot of the more violent physical contact; modern water polo resembles soccer more than it does rugby. Each team has a goalie and six swimmers, who push or pass the ball up the pool and try to throw it into a goal about 10 feet high and 3 feet wide.

It's an incredibly demanding sport, as players are forced to tread water at least 6 feet deep for the entire time (Croatian rules demand 10-minute quarters, 25 percent longer than those of any other country in the world) and must be ready to explode out of the water to shoot on goal or block an attacker. Play is still physical; it's just that most of the roughhousing goes on underneath the surface instead of above it. And the increased length of games isn't the only extra-difficult thing about Croatian water polo—many of the matches are played not in traditional pools but in seaside tidal pools that have been cordoned off to regulation size, which means waves, undertow, and the occasional fish. It's no wonder that Croatian players are among the best in the world.

POSTCARD FROM CROATIA

On the other side of the hill, I guess there is still a war going on, but you'd never know it in Dubrovnik, a peaceful, picturesque walled city on what looks like California coastline. Unlike in California, the architecture dates back centuries.

There's no real industry along the water, aside from cultivating mussels and oysters on ropes—the same way they've been doing it since the days of Alexander the Great—meaning the ocean is as pristine and pollution free as any in the world. No wonder it's a favorite stop for seagoing tourists; the crew and I wound up partying with a bunch of college kids visiting as part of their semester at sea.

The city may be the birthplace of the modern necktie, suggesting business, but Dubrovnik's soul belongs to the artists, who take over for nearly 7 weeks every summer, staging nightly plays, concerts, operas, and dance recitals. When the artists want to express their more athletic side, they turn to water polo.

If you want to get an understanding of water polo's popularity in Croatia, start with this: Some matches in Dubrovnik draw 5,000 spectators. That may not seem like a lot, until you realize that it's more than one-ninth of the population. It would be like a quarter-million Cincinnatians coming to see a Bengals game.

In my mind, there is a relationship between art and football. Both are crafts that demand a lot of practice and discipline, but offer many moments of free expression.

I'm used to practicing my craft on land. If I was going to succeed at water polo, keeping the art metaphor going for a moment longer, I was going to have to learn to use a different medium: the water.

Dubrovnik's hometown team, VK Jug, are the Yankees of Croatian water polo, only more successful: They've won the national championship eight times in the past 10 years and the world championship in 2007. There was no way I was going to get into a game with Yankees, but we found Gusar Mlini—Croatian for "the Pirates of Mlini Beach"—a second-division team that was willing to give me a shot.

There wasn't anything second-division about the workouts. Thirty minutes of swim sprints, followed by practice, followed by scrimmage. I can swim just fine, but this was about treading water. Let me tell you something: Muscle doesn't float. It takes a lot of damn work to beat my legs hard enough to keep my head above water.

The coach was an old-school screamer, his face perpetually disgusted, who wasn't inclined to cut any breaks (or playing time) just because I was a guest.

And did I mention we were playing in the ocean?

The pool was built into the side of the beach. There was a dividing wall that separated us from the ocean, but we still felt every wave, warm and cold currents, and, occasionally, a small fish who had happened to find his way over the wall.

I was exhausted beyond belief and, as a beginner to this particular medium, not very good.

—————

As if humiliating myself in the pool wasn't enough, I had to do the same on land.

The segment sounded easy: I was going to visit the top of Mount Srdj, one of Dubrovnik's highest peaks, to get a bird's-eye view of the city, and I wasn't even going to have to walk.

Ten years ago, I could have taken the cable car to the top, a slow ride with spectacular views, but it had been destroyed by the war. Instead, I was going to take an even slower route on the back of a donkey.

When we arrived at the meet-up with the donkey handler, however, we got some bad news. The donkeys had escaped. Maybe they heard a rumor about having to carry a 235-pound football player up a hill.

We spent an hour trudging through the brush, looking for the lost animals. I declared myself a "donkey whisperer," calling out in English, Croatian, and Donkey ("Hee-haw!") in a tone I was sure they'd respond to.

The donkeys were smarter than that. They knew who the real ass was. They stayed hidden.

We were on the verge of cancelling the bit when the donkey-wrangler cried out. He'd managed to find a few of the beasts hiding behind a bunch of trees. I climbed aboard one.

Donkeys are pretty ridiculous-looking animals. Sticking a large black man on a small donkey's back looked even more ridiculous. Apparently the donkey thought so, too—he refused to move, no matter what kind of treats he was offered.

We tried a second donkey. Same result. What's that they say about donkeys being stubborn?

Then again, so were we. The handler dragged that poor animal up the side of the hill with me on its back. I may have looked more foolish in my life, but I can't remember when.

When tourists go to New York City, they go see the Empire State Building and the Statue of Liberty. Visit a museum or two, meander through Central Park, maybe take in a Broadway show.

You'll get to see New York, but it's not what the locals do, at least not on a regular basis. To see the city like a New Yorker does, you would ditch the guidebooks and go to bars and clubs, restaurants and parties, spending your time interacting with the people who live there.

One night in Dubrovnik, we heard about a rave that was supposed to go down in a particular quarter of the city. A chance to experience the city the way the locals might. The trick was to find the party.

Dubrovnik doesn't have numbered streets or any gridlike organization; it's basically a labyrinth built into a hillside. Without a local to guide you, it's hard as hell to find anything, and ridiculously easy to get lost.

We didn't have a local to guide us.

Somehow we managed to find our way to the area of the city where the rave was supposed to take place. As we got closer, we could hear the music thumping. The problem was that the thumping was coming from the other side of a stone wall that had survived centuries of warfare. There was no obvious way to get to the other side.

If you can't go through something, go around it. We followed the wall to the city's docks, followed the docks to the beaches, and the beaches to the rocky jetties that surround the city. At times it felt like we were risking serious injury clambering over wet rocks on a nearly moonless night, but we were going to find this party if it killed us.

And suddenly, there it was. A DJ spinning records, speakers pounding bass, hundreds of people dancing in the streets, tweaking on God-knows-what. We joined the party and danced until the sun came up.

It's not always easy to get off the tourist trail, but it's the only way to create the kind of memories that you can't find in a guidebook.

———

If you want to learn an art, it's best to study at the feet of a master. I found that master in the form of Maro Joković.

Maro started playing water polo when he was 7. By the time he was 14, he was playing for VK Jug—the "Yankees" I mentioned earlier. Ten years later, he's still their star right wing. He represented Croatia in the last Olympics.

Maro taught me that there was a different way to move in the water that wasn't necessarily instinctive to a land-based mammal like me. Keep your left arm out, it will help you float. Move it forward, and you'll rise out of the water. Lean backwards, and your shots will fly high. Lean forward, and you can fire perfect bullets toward the goal. He showed me how to churn my legs like an eggbeater to tread water.

So I donned my tiny uniform—a bikini bottom that was frankly closer to a belt than a brief, putting my own frank and beans on full display—and prepared to play in a match with my fellow Croatian pirates.

It was only an exhibition game against a group of former water polo all-stars, but it still drew a huge crowd. There were cheerleaders. Pride was on the line—so much so that the coach kept me on the bench for most of the game.

In the second half, the coach looked my way. My turn. Time to scramble some eggs.

Someone passed me the ball in front of the net. I could hear the crowd screaming at me to shoot. So I did . . .

. . . straight into the goalie's arms. A second shot missed as well. The crowd murmured in disappointment. The coach was more blatant with his disappointment, removing me from the game.

But with just a few minutes left, Coach pulled me off the bench again and threw me back into the pool. I'd been given a second chance, and when I got the ball in front of the net, I rose out of the water like Maro had shown me, leaned forward, and fired a shot that skipped off the water into the goal.

One success, but that's what keeps us going amidst all the difficulties and failures that we experience in whatever craft we're trying to master.

EGGBEATERS

Swimming is normally considered active recovery—a low-stress way to move your muscles that will help you recover for the next "real" workout. But water polo isn't swimming. One of the most important skills you have to master is the ability to churn your legs—a motion called "the eggbeater"—to keep yourself afloat for the entire game.

You can try it in the deep end of any pool; just churn your legs in a circular motion for as long as you can. You'll get a cardiovascular workout, just like swimming, but you'll also be building a lot of new muscle fiber in your hips in a way that is really hard to duplicate.

Stronger hips mean more explosive tackles. Another day in Dhani's World Gym.

The Ties That Bind

What are the things that bring people together?

There's family, of course, and conversation. Politics, although that's just as likely to drive people apart. But I'm talking about large groups of people, hundreds of thousands of people, coming together on a regular basis.

Culture and sports.

The biggest festivals, outside of a few political gatherings, revolve around music, food, and sports. These events seem so basic: It's just about eating food, listening to some great sounds, or rooting for guys to push a ball around a field. Yet these simple activities are the ones that attract over 100,000 people on a regular basis.

Why? Because people get passionate about their food, culture, and music. And passion is an emotion that's best when it's shared.

High Passion
(Scotland)

Call it a dress. I dare you.

It's a kilt. Tell a Scotsman he's wearing a skirt, and as likely as not you're going to get punched in the face. It's what you might expect from a country whose motto roughly translates to "No one ticks me off and gets away with it."

The Scots are, let's say, a wee bit *passionate* when it comes to their culture.

Then again, when that culture's history goes back 13,000 years, I guess there's a lot to be passionate about.

The kilt isn't just a piece of clothing. For hundreds of years, those tartan patterns were your *colors,* defining your clan affiliation like Crips and Bloods—if the Crips and Bloods had been going at it for centuries instead of decades.

The Scots don't just play music—they've got the bagpipe. It's an incredibly complicated instrument, both to make and to play, with an unmistakable sound that used to inspire warriors to lay down their lives in battle.

They don't just drink—they drink Scotch. That'd be like us drinking "American." Only Scotch is much more important than that—it's *whiskey,* from the Scottish *uisge beatha.* Translation: "water of life."

They don't just have heroes—they have William Wallace, the original Rambo.

And the Scots don't just play games—they have the Highland Games, one of the most spectacular displays of strength, speed, dexterity, heritage, and, yes, *passion* that human beings have been able to invent.

THE HIGHLAND GAMES

People have been living in the Scottish Highlands since prehistoric times. There's plenty of evidence to suggest that they've been competing in sports there for just as long.

No one knows exactly how old the Highland Games are. A lot of Scots like to say that the official beginning was in the 11th century, when the king of Scotland held a race to find the fastest man in his country, so that he could enlist him as the royal messenger.

Ever since, the Games have been a forum for Scotsmen to establish themselves and their clans in the eyes of their society, proving their worth as athletes and warriors while celebrating a sense of Scottish pride. Which they've had to—Scotland has been fighting off invaders for as long as there has been history: the Romans, the English, the English again. Even after the Scots made peace with England to form Great Britain, the Scottish Highlanders still had to fight off attacks from their new countrymen.

The Highland Games represent a response to the endless history of attacks:

We're still here.

The Games are full of pageantry—parades, bagpipes, traditional costumes, and dancing. It's said that they provided inspiration for the modern-day Olympics.

There are still events to determine the fastest man in the land. But the center stage is dedicated to men in kilts performing massive feats of strength: throwing heavy stones and hammers, tossing weights for distance and height, and the granddaddy of them all, the caber toss.

This is roughly equivalent to lifting a telephone pole out of the ground and tossing it end over end, à la the Incredible Hulk.

———————————

When I learn a new sport, there's usually a pretty set formula. I watch, learn the moves, practice, and execute. Along the way, I might learn something about the sport's traditions, history, or culture.

In Scotland, that equation was flipped on its head. I'd learn the moves, but first I was going to have to master the tradition behind them.

My coach, Gregor Edmunds, was a former World Highland Games champion. He began my training by explaining his lineage: Gregor's father had been the world caber-tossing champion.

Then Gregor took me to get fitted for a kilt. I had to dress for the Games before I could play in the Games.

When we finally got around to training, he took me to Braemar, the place where the Highland Games are rumored to have originated, a gathering place for the Scottish clans to compete until it was outlawed by the English in the 18th century. The ban didn't last long, and today Braemar is home to an annual competition on the first Saturday of September.

To the Scots, Braemar is hallowed ground. It was the place, Gregor told me, where his father wanted to someday have his ashes scattered.

My history lesson didn't end there. Gregor unlocked a storage area underneath the grandstands, revealing a collection of some of the Games' most legendary cabers. It was like visiting a secret room at Yankee Stadium so that Derek Jeter could teach you how to hit with a bat that once belonged to Mickey Mantle.

"Caber" comes from the Gaelic word for "tree trunk," which is an entirely accurate description—they're tree trunks, almost 20 feet long, that weigh about 175 pounds. The object is to lift the caber, somehow balance it on your shoulder, gather some forward momentum, and toss it. A successful throw gets enough height and distance for the caber to flip, plant its topside on the ground, and fall neatly into a 12 o'clock position.

I didn't come anywhere near a successful throw.

The next thing I learned is that rookie caber tossers were responsible for making their own cabers. Gregor took me to a farm near the woods. We cut down a tree, fed it into a machine that skimmed off the bark and branches, and used a chain saw to taper the ends.

I hoped that having my own caber would somehow improve my proficiency. But after 3 more hours of practice—see Dhani lift the caber; see Dhani run from the caber; see Dhani curse a blue streak—my producers pulled the plug. They loved seeing me miserable, but there wasn't enough light left to shoot. I was tired, pissed off, and no closer to a successful throw.

The next day, I spent the morning practicing the hammer throw with Grant Anderson, another former champion. He showed me how to use special cleats to clamp my feet to the ground—otherwise, the momentum generated by swinging a 22-pound hammer around my head might lead me to seriously hurt myself. Or kill an innocent bystander.

This practice was slightly more successful: I was able to throw the hammer approximately 75 feet. It was less than half the distance of Grant's world record throw, but I was a little more confident that I wasn't going to accidentally kill anybody.

Everything I saw in Scotland was rooted in tradition.

I went to a bagpipe factory, which wasn't like any kind of factory I'd ever seen: Everything was still done by hand, with careful craftsmanship. A finished bagpipe involved 11 steps by 5 different workers in 3 different rooms.

We visited a Scotch distillery. Americans drink beer that gets churned out of vats by the gallon. The Scots drink a whiskey that's been malted from a single barley and aged for years in wooden casks that used to store sherry, giving it a distinctive fire and flavor.

I helped a butcher make haggis, Scotland's take on the "let's use the whole animal" philosophy. He showed me how to stuff a ground lamb, plus its liver and lungs, onions, oatmeal, and huge chunks of fat, into a piece of intestine. Haggis is still favored by a lot of Highland Games champions, thanks to its reputation for making you stronger and more potent. It might also explain Gregor's gas, the odor of which was championship quality.

(Which begs the question: Why is everything that is disgusting supposed to make us strong or virile? Bugs, goat's eye, or any other nasty shit that I've had to eat, someone is always telling me that it will improve my potency. I guess it's the best way to get men to eat anything. Probably what mothers had to do to get their kids to eat. "Eat this, boy. It will help you go longer with your woman!")

All the places I visited had one thing in common: They were driven by pride rather than efficiency. There are probably easier ways to make bagpipes; there are definitely easier instruments to play. There are faster ways to get drunk than waiting 20 years for a Scotch to mellow, and tastier ways to prepare lamb. But in Scotland, it's not about doing things the easiest way. It's about doing things the Scottish way.

I didn't win the Highland Games.

I didn't even come close. My best result was a seventh-place finish in the stone put.

Losing is not part of my nature. It doesn't feel right to get a pat on the back for trying. But maybe that was the lesson that Scotland was trying to teach me: You win some, you lose some, but the most important thing is to stay proud.

WEIGHT FOR HEIGHT

All the events I tried in the Highland Games forced me to move heavy weights around in a way my body wasn't used to—a great way to build strength. My favorite was called "weight for height."

The heavy version had me holding a 56-pound weight with an attached handle, but you can use whatever weight you feel comfortable with. Starting from a squatting position, with my left hand resting on my left leg, I swung my right arm—the one holding the weight—toward the sky. Exploding from the squat, I released the weight, trying to throw it high enough to clear a bar. My best toss made it over a bar that was 13 feet high.

The unique motion worked my legs, core, shoulders, back, and arm (both arms if you switch hands) in a way that was a lot more satisfying than a Soloflex.

You probably don't want to be in the gym tossing 50-pound weights into the air, but there are always opportunities for exercise around you. Pick up a rock and carry it for a while. Run up the stairs instead of taking the elevator.

How do the Scots get better at tossing the caber? By tossing the fucking caber! And the best way to get more athletic is to always be an athlete.

Even Buffaloes Have to Nap

I love the excitement of travel. Can't imagine living without it. It's hard, sometimes, to remember that it's my hobby, not my day job.

A lot of football players use their off-season to catch up on rest. Not me. Being on the road doesn't leave much time for relaxation.

Changing time zones can wreak havoc on my internal clock. There's no letup once we've arrived at a place: Wakeup is at 6:00 a.m.—unless it's earlier.

Football comes first, so I've usually worked out for 2 hours before I've even started thinking about what I'm going to do in a new country. When I was shooting the show, we'd generally have a quick breakfast and be in the van by 9:00. An hour of travel time, then another 2 hours for whatever sport we were practicing. Lunch, filming, possibly another workout. Dinner, then maybe an additional night bit or a drink with the crew. Some treatment for my sore body—acupuncture, massage, whatever—then bed. Wake up and do it again the next day.

Tired? I don't get tired. Relaxation? I sleep in vans and on planes. (Apologies for the snoring.) I sleep during acupuncture treatments—not so easy when someone's sticking 200 pins into your body. A woman gives me a scalp massage, I'm hers for all of about 5 minutes. Then I'll probably fall asleep.

If I have my way, even my sleep is productive. I remember as a kid falling asleep during concerts at the Kennedy Center. For me, it was like sleeping on a biology book—something has to get absorbed. Pretty sure that's how I learned to conduct a symphony.

I might sleep with an ice pack, a heating pad, or a compression machine to help my body heal during the "downtime."

There's a saying I like—I'm not sure if it's Native American or something I made up when I was half-asleep—but I'm thinking about getting it tattooed on my side:

As a buffalo roams alone, so shall you find peace in the comfort of death.

To be completely honest, I don't know exactly what it means. But I feel like it describes my life perfectly. It's not (I hope) saying that I have a death wish, because nothing could be further from the truth. I love life. I love living life. I just don't build a lot of rest and relaxation into my plans.

The nice part about living this way? When I do wind up taking a couple of days off to let my body recover, or I find myself in a place where I can party for a couple of days, I appreciate it all the more.

But not for long.

The buffalo needs to start roaming again.

Everyt'ing Criss
(Jamaica)

When people think of Jamaica, they often start with Bob Marley, marijuana smoke, dreadlocks, and Rastafarians. Yes, there is a lot of pot being smoked in Jamaica. And everyone I met loved them some Bob Marley. But I was surprised to discover that there aren't that many Rastafarians—most Jamaicans are practicing Christians.

As part of the episode we filmed there, we visited a church to take in an evening service. For the first hour or so, it wasn't very different from the church I grew up with. People read from the Bible, praised God, and sang the familiar hymns.

Then the African drums kicked in.

Suddenly, everybody was dancing. Some of the women were shaking, as if possessed by a spirit—not in a Baptist-revival, celebratory, praise-Jesus kind of way, but in the Caribbean let's-kick-the-evil-spirits-out-of-our-bodies kind of way. The African way.

The Jamaicans had taken Christianity and made it their own.

You could see the same dynamic played out on the cricket field. There may not be a tamer, more civilized, more gentlemanly—let's call it what it is: *white*—game than cricket. Just don't tell that to the Jamaicans, who have appropriated the game from their former colonial masters and made it their own.

CRICKET

They say the use of tools is what separates us from the apes. Cavemen figured out how to use sticks to beat on their prey. Some of the more fun-loving ones figured out how to play with a ball. Somewhere along the line, folks started using the sticks to hit the balls.

But it took the English to formalize this activity into a game sometime during the Middle Ages. Not just any Englishmen, but kings and prep-schoolers. And not just any game, but an incredibly complicated sport with baffling rules whose matches could go on for days at a time.

On a basic level, there are two teams, 11 players per side. Each team gets a chance to bat—sometimes twice, depending on the rules—and tries to score as many runs as possible. The other team tries to prevent them from scoring. The team that scores the most runs wins.

Simple, right? But from there, it starts to get weird.

There are 10 different ways to get a batter out, or "dismissed," most of them revolving around knocking one of two wooden crossbars (the "bails") off its perch on the top of three closely arranged sticks in the ground (the "wicket"). A "bowler" gets six chances to fire, gently arc, roll, or even bounce a ball past the batter, hoping to hit the wicket, dislodging the bail. The batter keeps batting for as long as he's able to protect the wicket (or gets dismissed for one of several other reasons too complicated to address here), driving in runs with hits. Depending on the type of hit, it can be worth anywhere from one to six runs. A skilled batter may survive against dozens of bowlers, leading to games that can go on for several days.

The English love the game—there have been professional cricket players since the 17th century. As the British Empire expanded around the world, they brought cricket with them, introducing it to Australia, New Zealand, South Africa, India, Pakistan, and the West Indies in an effort to bring some "civilization" to the locals. For the English, cricket is, above all, a gentleman's game, valuing sportsmanship and proper manners above unseemly competitiveness, showmanship, or other bad behavior. Most of the countries that adopted cricket have maintained the gentlemanly sensibility: The continuing rivalry between India and Pakistan, whose televised matches often attract nearly a billion viewers, may very well be the major reason the two countries haven't yet resorted to nuclear war.

In the West Indies, the game was mainly an opportunity for homesick Englishmen to enjoy a taste of home. That is, until the 1960s, when black people were allowed to start playing the game.

Good-bye, crumpets and tea; hello, jerk chicken and Red Stripe.

Set to a Caribbean beat, cricket was suddenly infused with a heaping pile of attitude, trash-talking, flamboyance, self-expression, and athleticism. For the locals, the game was an opportunity to overcome stereotypes and lingering feelings of inferiority. By the 1970s, the "Windies," as they were called, were totally dominating the international scene.

Cricket is still huge in the islands, especially Jamaica, where kids play it in the streets the way Americans play basketball. The rules are basically as convoluted as ever, but the spirit is pure Jamaica.

POSTCARD FROM JAMAICA

Montego Bay. Ocho Rios. That's where the cruise ships come in, so that's where most people go. Tourists imagine the rest of Jamaica as a blaxploitation version of the Wild West: danger, violence, and bullets flying everywhere.

There is some truth to Jamaica's rep. The murder rate is high. Seems like everybody I meet carries a knife. But the only way to see the real country is to get out of the tourist mentality—and the tourist areas—to see the cities, like Kingston, or the rural countryside, like St. Ann's Parish, birthplace of Bob Marley.

It's a lush, beautiful country, where British culture and African passion have merged with a laid-back island sensibility. It's not a big country, but damn if it hasn't changed the world with its music (reggae), its cuisine (can't get enough jerk chicken!), and the unmistakable Jamaican patois (especially funny when you hear it spoken by a local of white or Chinese descent). Maybe it's all the grass being smoked, but no one seems to be in too much of a hurry. And while there's plenty of poverty, most people aren't letting it get them down. "Everyt'ing criss," as they say. Everything is right with the world.

———————————————

I didn't think I was going to like cricket. The game moves at a slow pace. A *slo-o-o-o-ow* pace, even when played with a couple of Jamaican twists designed to shorten the games from several days to several hours. There were hundreds of rules that I didn't understand, or care to.

My guide, local cricket legend Jimmy Adams, took me to the game's heartland, Bull Savanna, where he tried to teach me the "basics." I thought my head was going to explode.

But when you want to know the truth about something, you ask a kid. Jamaican kids love cricket.

Jimmy took me to Kingston, where he helps keep the children *on* the street—playing cricket—and out of trouble. I finally got to see the game played the Jamaican way.

The kids were merciless, mocking me for my lack of skill, screaming at me when I forgot a rule (like holding on to my bat as I ran from one wicket to another).

They were also incredibly creative, using two-by-fours and tennis balls instead of costly regulation gear. When a ball got hit on the roof of a nearby building, it wasn't lost or even out of play: I watched a kid scale the wall, quickly track down the ball, and throw a perfect strike from the roof to knock the bail off the wicket. Batter out!

This wasn't the boring sport I'd imagined. This was *resistance* cricket: aggressive, athletic, flamboyant, and fun.

Color me hooked.

Even though Jamaicans play with a lot more athleticism than the British who introduced the game, cricket isn't exactly a sport that demands athleticism. Like an American softball game, there are plenty of beer bottles set along the foul lines for easy access. I practiced batting, fielding, and bowling, but I wasn't exactly exerting myself.

I still did my football workouts in the morning, but after the strength workouts in Ireland and Scotland and the exhausting aerobics of Italy and Croatia, they felt a lot easier than I remembered.

We travelled the country to shoot the show, but we travelled at a Jamaican pace. No choice but. The drivers were slow. The restaurants were slow. "In time, mon, in time" seemed to be the national motto.

My biggest stress in Jamaica was the fear that all the secondhand smoke I was inhaling—even old ladies were blowing it in my face, confused as to why I wouldn't partake—was going to earn me a suspension from the NFL.

The second-biggest stress was all the teasing I took. Cricket wasn't a game where I could style and profile. Didn't matter at all that I was a professional athlete—you're either good at the game or you're not.

My skills were weak. Jimmy and his friends made fun of my blisters, clearly a sign of my soft hands. They told me I swung like a girl. I thought it was hilarious. I hear a lot worse on the football field.

In other words, Jamaica was doing its best to make sure that any stress melted away.

Jamaica wasn't doing anything at all. I had to slow down. I had to relax. I had to tap into the energy, which is to save your energy for a moment when you might need it. A moment that may never come.

At the end of the week, I joined Jimmy and his friends in a match between Bull Savanna and rival Watchwell. I spent most of the game lying under a tree while Jimmy tore up the opposition, single-handedly driving in 47 of the 89 runs we scored.

Defense was a little more of an adventure—after some beginner's luck, my lack of bowling skills and my suspect hands were exposed in the field. We got shelled. Our huge lead evaporated and we lost by three runs.

Didn't matter. Everyt'ing was still criss.

Passive Recovery

It's Jamaica, mon. No matter how active you are, sometimes nothing is the only thing to do. While I might not have been able to relax in the Jamaican style—toking a fat spliff—the good vibes I received from everyone around me were relaxation enough.

Cincinnati, Part Two

My first year in Cincinnati, I didn't bother with a car. I lived in a hotel only a few blocks from the stadium. I wanted to focus on football, on reviving my career. So I bought a bike, put my head down, and pedaled to and from work.

One day, riding up Vine Street, I lifted my head up and saw something that surprised me:

A lot of tall buildings.

Not just any tall buildings, but corporate headquarters. Procter & Gamble. Macy's. Kroger's. Fifth Third Bank.

It might not be in-your-face, like New York City, but maybe, quietly, something was going on in Cincinnati after all.

One of the keys to restarting my career in Cincinnati was to show my coaches that I cared. I wanted them to understand that my travels weren't just about taking a break from football (although that was part of it), but were helping me to become a better football player.

So I invited them along. Two of them took the bait.

The first was my linebacker coach, Jeff Fitzgerald. I've had good relationships with a lot of coaches, but Coach Fitz was one of the first who, in my eyes, saw me as a complete person. The first time we met, at the Potato Shack in Encinitas, California, we spoke for about 30 minutes about football. Then we spent the next 2 hours talking about travel.

It wasn't too hard to get Coach Fitz to meet me in Croatia. We talked a lot of football and went over the playbook, while he got a first-hand look at how hard I was working.

On my next stop, Scotland, Brent Rogers came to meet me. Brent isn't with the team anymore—he's moved on to a bigger job at the College of Mount St. Joseph—but at the time, he was one of the Bengals' assistant strength coaches. Brent got to see me work out with the Scots while taking me through a few football workouts of his own. We didn't have a traditional gym to work with, so we trained in the woods with large rocks that we recovered from a river.

I wanted the team to know that I felt connected to them, and for them to feel connected to me.

The path of least resistance may be the easiest, but it doesn't spur new growth or allow new things to happen.

The 2009 season was all about struggle, beginning with our very first game. We banged heads with the Denver Broncos, keeping them to just two field goals over the first 59 minutes. We stuffed their running game and kept them under 200 yards passing. The Broncos had done a little better, making a couple of key interceptions and keeping us from scoring at all. But with 38 seconds left, we finally managed to scrape out a touchdown, taking the lead at 7-6. All we had to do was hold them.

The Broncos tried a desperation pass. One of our cornerbacks, Leon Hall, got to it first, tipping it away—and into the hands of a Denver receiver who sped 87 yards down the field for the game-winning touchdown. It was a fluke play that helped make the TV announcer who called it, Gus Johnson, a household name. It will live on in NFL highlight reels for years to come. Just not our highlight reel.

There was personal adversity. In September, a tsunami hit American Samoa. Several of my teammates had family there. Three weeks later, the wife of Mike Zimmer, our defensive coordinator, died unexpectedly. The sense of loss pervaded our locker room.

Our sense of resiliency, however, turned out to be stronger than ever. We won our next four games with come-from-behind victories.

Suddenly, the sports media didn't see us as losers anymore. We were the "Cardiac Cats," a scrappy team with a penchant for late-game heroics.

We swept and won our division, the AFC North, and made the playoffs for the first time in five seasons. Marvin Lewis was named Coach of the Year. On a personal level, I had my best season since my days with the Giants, leading the team in tackles and setting a career high in sacks.

Turnarounds belong to everyone involved, and everyone on the team was involved. It's impossible to point to just one aspect of the team to account for our change in fortune.

But for me, the team's rebirth felt like part of my own process of revitalizing my life.

The Perfect Woman

A little while back, I was on a radio show and was asked to describe my perfect woman.

I didn't have to think too hard, because I already know who she is. Or who I want her to be, anyway. I carry a list of her qualities around on my BlackBerry.

She's tall and slender, with long hair, incredible hands, and insatiable eyes. Exotic features, maybe light brown or olive skin.

Smart and quick-witted, but also in possession of a calming, motherly quality. She wants a huge family.

Adventurous, sporty, and looking to live life.

Strong and independent. She's okay on her own but loves her man and stands firm behind him.

Has a huge heart and a creative soul.

Well-travelled. Speaks languages other than her own. Maybe she doesn't even live in the States. I'm willing to move for her—Brazil, London, North Africa, South Africa, New Zealand, New York. I'll spend time wherever she is.

And she cooks.

Not surprisingly, I took a lot of shit for having a list.

People said my standards were too high, even after I explained this was really more of a guideline, that the "perfect woman" only had to have about 75 percent of those qualities to make me happy.

My problem is that I know this woman exists!

My sister plays every sport. She's married, has two kids, and takes care of the house, cooking, cleaning, doing the laundry. She speaks some Spanish and works from home. When they go to the airport, she carries the tickets.

My mom's not the greatest athlete, but she plays tennis all the time. She's a prodigy, a physician who also raised two kids. She took care of the house, even if she occasionally paid somebody to clean it. Her list of friends reads like roll call at the United Nations.

Yes, I have high expectations. Why shouldn't I have high expectations for the person I'm supposed to spend my life with? I refuse to be the unhappily wedded man, the guy who dreads coming home, who exalts the next stripper he runs into who will give him a hand job.

I want to wake up every morning and be like, "Damn! How the hell did I end up with *you*? Why did you like me?"

It Takes All Types
(Brazil)

I wasn't always privy to the conversations going on behind the scenes that led my TV producers to choose one place over another. Usually I had to guess. Sometimes I thought it had to do with a specific kind of challenge, like England, where we tried to settle the question of which sport was tougher, rugby or football. Other times, it felt more circumstantial—New Zealand, for example, was suggested by the Travel Channel because they had a relationship with the country's tourism board. A lot of the time, I thought it came down to the visuals. Rolling hills, lush landscapes, and exotic seascapes all look good on television.

Or in the case of Brazil, beautiful bodies.

I'm not saying that volleyball isn't a real sport. It's definitely a real and very challenging sport, one that requires a sick level of fitness, quick reflexes, and explosiveness.

What I am saying is that, in my mind, the concept that drew us to playing volleyball in Rio de Janeiro could roughly be summed up as "beautiful beaches, beautiful bodies, against the backdrop of Carnival."

Not that there was anything wrong with that.

BEACH VOLLEYBALL

Volleyball began in the United States as an indoor game, something to do in a gymnasium, or maybe one of the new YMCAs that were popping up all over the place during the 1800s. But it took a group of Hawaiian surfers, killing time between waves, to figure out that the game would work just as well on the beach. Maybe even better.

The idea quickly spread east to Southern California, where beach volleyball sparked a revolution that would ultimately sweep around the world, even to places that don't have beaches—the headquarters for the sport's international governing body is in landlocked Switzerland. Beach volleyball has been an Olympic sport since 1996.

If you've ever taken a gym class at school, then you probably already know the basic rules: Knock the ball over the net, without catching or throwing it, and make your opponents miss. First team to score 21 points wins the game.

Beach volleyball is generally played two-on-two, and teammates are allowed to pass the ball back and forth up to three times before hitting it over the net. On offense, the strategy usually involves one player using her fingertips (a "set shot") or wrists (a "bump") to put the ball in a position where her teammate can slam it over the net (a "spike"). Defensive players, who often communicate using secret hand signals behind their backs, try to position themselves to block potential spikes while limiting the exposed terrain where a shot might land.

It's fast-paced and exciting, accounting for some of its popularity. It's also played by scantily clad people with incredibly athletic bodies, which should explain the rest.

POSTCARD FROM RIO

The Portuguese who landed in Rio de Janeiro thought they'd found Eden. It's not hard to see why: Very few places on earth have such a crazy mix of scenic topography—towering mountains, thick rain forests, spectacular beaches—in such a limited space. Even Rio's poorest areas—the impoverished mountainside favelas—are built on landscape that people in California would pay millions for.

The "mix" theme runs throughout the city. A third of the population describes itself as multiracial, incorporating ethnicities as remote as the Middle East and China. Rio is grounded in religion—Cristo Redentor, a 130-foot-tall statue of Jesus, watches over the city—but is also one of the most open-minded cultures in the world when it comes to sexuality and dress.

It's the beaches, however, where the city's vibrancy is really on display, blending the qualities of a spiritual sanctuary, a lively social club, a restaurant with a great view, and an open-air gym. No wonder that it's ritual for beachgoers to applaud each sunset, thanking the powers above for providing such a daily miracle.

I was going to learn how to play volleyball on Ipanema Beach—as in, "The Girl from . . ." I had visions of gorgeous ladies with exotic features splashing in the surf, wearing nearly nothing, impressed as all get-out by my volleyball prowess.

I wasn't disappointed, at least not by the ladies. The beaches were as sexy as advertised. I was surrounded by beautiful bodies everywhere, in swimsuits that would have raised a lot of eyebrows in the States. But I was just as impressed by the bodies that, under different circumstances, I might not have described as beautiful.

Brazilians love the human body in whatever form it happens to take. Self-expression is as important as any idea of classical beauty or "perfect" features.

This kind of open-mindedness is all over Rio, especially its beaches. The various lifeguard stations, or *postos,* attract different social groups. Posto 9, once a symbol of Rio's counterculture, is now a meeting place for trendy hipsters from around the world. Posto 8 is a place for Rio's lively gay culture to thrive.

A lively culture it is. Our hotel in Rio was in a neighborhood so gay that even gay people thought it was gay. Homosexuals, transvestites, transgender, trans-everybody: It's all readily accepted in Rio. Didn't bother me—live and let live, as far as I'm concerned—even if I did occasionally feel like a piece of man-meat on my walks to the beach.

But Rio isn't just about open-mindedness: It's about constant reinvention. Many graffiti artists are considered just that—artists, beautifying that which was already there.

The city's most famous set of stairs might be the Escadaria Selarón. Twenty years ago, a Chilean-born artist named Jorge Selarón looked at the run-down staircase near his house and saw a canvas. He began covering the steps with homemade tiles. You can find Selarón doing exactly the same thing today: The 250 stairs are decorated with over 2,000 tiles from 60 different countries. He took a break to explain to me that he considers the stairs to be an evolving work of art—when he finishes working on an area, he moves to another that he's already completed, retiling it to suit his current mind-set.

The project will be finished, he said, on the day he dies.

Selarón also paints. I wound up buying one of his paintings. It didn't occur to me until I got to the airport that I had no way to bring it with me on the plane. I wound up giving it to one of our tour guides, who still swears up and down that she's going to figure out a way to send it to me.

I'm not holding my breath. Maybe it's a lesson. One of the great truths about travelling is that you can't always take what you find back home with you.

———

Our visit coincided with Carnival, Rio's famous (and occasionally infamous) 4-day street fair that dates back nearly 3 centuries. It's a time when free expression is celebrated and elevated into a national art form. The highlight of the festival is the Carnival Parade, an unforgettable gathering of dancing people, intricate costumes, and surreal floats.

The parading people usually belong to samba schools, social clubs that revolve around Brazil's national form of dance. Like everything else in Brazil, samba is a fusion of influences, combining indigenous South American traditions with European and African rhythms. And also like everything else in Brazil, there's no "right" way to do it— everyone who dances the samba makes it his or her own. It's all about relaxing and letting go.

I hooked up with one of Rio's most famous samba schools, Grêmio Recreativo Escola de Samba Mocidade Independente de Padre Miguel, or more simply, Mocidade. The group was formed in the 1950s by eight people who grew up in the neighborhood known as Padre Miguel; today there are more than 3,000 members from all over the place.

Each year, the group adopts a specific theme to inform its costumes and floats. During my visit, the idea was that paradise—the Garden of Eden—exists in each of us.

I joined hundreds of Mocidade members armed with scissors, glue guns, and sewing machines, using feathers, fabrics, gems, metals, and mirrors to help create their costumes and floats. That's how Carnival gets made. Nothing is mass-produced; it's produced by the masses, each person adding his or her individual sense of style and flair along the way.

A few days later, I danced with Mocidade through Carnival, dressed in the costume of a miner. I joined them in singing their school's anthem, which translates to:

My heart escapes from my mouth.
I cannot hold back this passion.
Independent light takes me up to the sky.
I am Mocidade.
I am Padre Miguel.

The song reminded me of another chant, maybe a little less eloquent, but spoken with just as much enthusiasm before many of our football games:

"Who dey! Who dey! Who dey think gonna beat dem Bengals?"

What is a football team, if not a collection of very distinct personalities defined by a particular neighborhood? Each season, a group of individuals combines their particular style and flair to form a costumed group, one that is in a constant state of reinvention, hoping that the sum of the talents adds up to create something larger and more enduring than the respective parts.

On every team I play for, I usually gravitate toward one employee who really takes care of me, rounding up all the little things I need to get through the season. During the previous year with the Bengals, that employee was Lamar. I thought about getting him a really nice Christmas gift. Instead, I hired him to be my trainer on the trip to Brazil.

Lamar couldn't have been more excited. It was his first time in Rio, and all he wanted to do was soak it in, seeing everything, meeting everybody. His generosity of spirit extended to the two female tour guides who were leading us around. When they needed to take showers one afternoon, he was happy to provide them with his hotel room.

In return, one of the guides was happy to answer Lamar's phone when it rang. Only problem was, it was Lamar's girlfriend.

"You got me in a mess with my girl!" Lamar complained to me. No good deed goes unpunished, as the expression goes. I spent the rest of the trip listening to his often hilarious agony over the best way to make amends.

Yes, there was a volleyball game. I practiced my ass off and did the best I could. My partner, Arturo, and I came within a point of victory, but wound up losing 22-20 to a couple of guys much more skilled than we were.

But it's not the volleyball I remember about Rio. It's the sense of individual freedom and self-expression combining to create something unexpected and always evolving.

That, and a lot of beautiful women in bikinis.

PLYOMETRIC TRAINING

Most training takes place on a fixed surface: a floor, a field, a mat. Ideally, the surface has a little give, so the repetitive nature of the training doesn't cause too much damage to your body.

But when you exercise on a surface with a lot of give, like sand, something very different happens. On a technical level, your muscles are reaching their maximum level of contraction in a shorter period of time. You may be more familiar with the effects on a personal level— running around in the sand tires you the hell out.

You're not just getting more tired, however—you're actually developing fast-twitch muscle fibers, improving your ability to move with explosiveness. Trainers call it "plyometrics," and it's particularly useful for developing a fast first step or a quicker leap.

So the next time you're at the beach, whether you're playing volleyball or just running after your kids, you'll actually be training like the professionals do.

Life Is Complicated,
Sports Are Simple

There are so many decisions to make in life. Only rarely are they clear-cut.

Take a left turn there, and wonder forever what would have happened had you gone right. Leave what you know to jump through a window, or watch it shut for good. Weigh the pluses and minuses, the pros and cons. The fish or the chicken. Paper or plastic.

It's a wonder we're able to decide anything at all.

Except for sports.

It's the first question everybody asks when they sit down to watch a game: "Who are you rooting for?" Suddenly all of life's difficult decisions slip away, replaced by something simple. Michigan or Ohio State? The Steelers or the Bengals?

And just as fast, the moment of serenity is gone. "What do you mean you don't like the Bengals? What is wrong with you? Get the hell out of here!"

Small Steps
(South Africa)

Soccer is a game of endurance, fast reflexes, and a surprising degree of physicality. For an American football player, so far, so good.

The trickiest difference, as it turns out, is learning how to take small steps. There's a time to sprint down the field at full speed, but when you've got the ball, those long strides aren't going to work. Small steps lead to long passes, and long passes can lead to goals.

South Africa was a completely different kind of Africa than I had experienced before. Unlike Senegal, rooted in its proud past, the vibe in South Africa was of a country moving away from its past—one small step at a time.

It's a country where no one quite feels at home, not yet anyway. Everyone is still dealing with the end of apartheid, which changed South Africa's dynamics without necessarily changing the emotions associated with them.

It's not even as simple as black and white. South Africa also makes distinctions for "coloured"—those people of mixed African and European or Asian ancestry, who make up nearly 10 percent of the population. Until apartheid ended, all three "races" had different laws and rights.

Diversity is an unshakable fact of South African life. Eleven different languages are used every day. The country has larger Asian and European populations than any other on the continent. In addition to the three races—and all the various tribes they belong to—there's an incredible biodiversity, including over 20,000 different plants; that's 10 percent of all the known plants in the world.

Everybody's trying to get along. But a quarter of the population is out of work, living on not much more than a dollar a day. Crime and AIDS are staggering problems. Prejudice and racism are still everywhere.

The situation is evolving and, we can hope, progressing.

But it's complicated, the kind of situation that makes you grateful for the simplicity of sports.

POSTCARD FROM SOUTH AFRICA

People have been living here for 100,000 years. It just hasn't been the same people.

Ancient African tribes battled over the land for centuries before the Europeans showed up a few hundred years ago. Once they discovered that the hills were full of diamonds and gold, they battled one another for control. The British finally won out, establishing a colony in 1806, planting the seeds of a system that would subjugate blacks for nearly 200 years.

Despite all the turmoil, it's easy to see why people fell in love with Cape Town. The climate resembles that of San Francisco, only slightly warmer, with more sunlight. There's a wind that blows through every summer, cleaning pollution from the air. A different kind of wind seems to be moving the country into a more progressive and just place, maybe not as quickly, but just as dramatically.

SOCCER

Soccer—really only a word that Americans use; it's "association football" to everyone else in the world—started in England, maybe as early as the 9th century, when mobs of people reputedly entertained themselves by kicking an inflated pig's bladder from one side of the village to the other.

A thousand years later, the rules were standardized to create the more modern form of the game that is far and away the most popular in the world. Over a quarter-billion people are said to play regularly.

The rules are fairly simple. Matches are played 11-on-11. Each team tries to move the ball up the field, called a "pitch," without using their hands, in the hopes of knocking it into a goal. Most of the work is done with the feet, but the chest and head play important roles as well. Matches usually have two 45-minute halves. At the end, the team with the most goals wins.

There were a lot of countries we could have chosen to try soccer. Pretty much any country. What was appealing about South Africa, aside from the natural beauty and compelling political and cultural story, was the upcoming 2010 World Cup. It would be the first time the tournament had been played on African soil, and South Africa was in a frenzy, building 10 new soccer stadiums and upgrading the country's infrastructure to handle the anticipated millions of foreign spectators.

It was clear what soccer meant to the country today. But I wanted to start with a slightly different perspective.

South Africa's system of apartheid—a set of laws designed to maintain the white minority's political and economic dominance over a black majority—ended in 1994. Getting there, however, had taken years of struggle.

About 4 miles off the coast of Cape Town lies Robben Island, once home to one of South Africa's most infamous prisons. Many of the people who spoke up against apartheid were, at one time or another, jailed here.

The island has since been converted to a museum. Many people visit to see the cell where apartheid's most famous opponent, Nelson Mandela, lived for 18 years.

My guide, Dede Ntsoelengoe—who was himself imprisoned at Robben Island for 7 years, beginning his sentence as a 14-year-old— couldn't have been more somber as he showed me the tiny space where

Mandela was housed. There was a blanket to sleep on, a tiny table, and a literal pot to piss in (also used to wash clothes), jammed into a space smaller than my closet.

But when we stepped outside into the yard, Dede's face lit up. "This is where we played soccer," he said.

Soccer wasn't just a form of exercise for the prisoners—it was the only place where they could experience a semblance of normal life. The players could talk freely. The guards became spectators. The crushing weight of history could be set aside, replaced by a game.

Dede and I kicked the ball back and forth for a while. It was humbling to play on a field where the fathers of South Africa's modern democracy found their peace.

"The first lesson of soccer," Dede said. "The ball is your friend."

It's good to have a friend in South Africa.

Great white sharks patrol the surrounding seas, picking off baby seals—and the occasional swimmer.

The country is full of wild animals. Most of them are relegated to wilderness areas, but even there you're better off not getting out of the car—get within 50 yards of a lion on foot, and you're toast. The deadliest animal, even more so than the rhinos, elephants, and leopards, might be the water buffalo, who will attack without warning.

During my safari trip into the wilderness, it was refreshing to see that not everything was dangerous. We caught a glimpse of elephants playing happily in their element. One of my guides convinced them to come over and hang out with us for a while.

Even in lethal lands, it's important to play.

Despite being a British import, soccer was considered by most South Africans to be mainly a "black" sport. The country's Premier Soccer League was founded shortly after apartheid's end.

I hooked up with Ajax Cape Town, a team formed to help feed international talent to the legendary Dutch team, AFC Ajax. My new teammates seemed like a microcosm of the dynamics that defined the country. Some of them showed up in their Mercedes. Others relied on the team snack, a muffin and a glass of milk, as their primary source of nourishment. Everybody was pretty friendly to one another on the pitch, but after practice there were some white players who would never think of giving one of their black teammates a ride home.

I followed one of my teammates to his home in the shantytowns of Cape Flats, where he grew up. It's one of the most violent places on earth: the most rapes and assaults per capita; second in murders. Gangs run the streets. In addition to massive unemployment, AIDS affects as many as one in five people, killing hundreds of thousands of South Africans each year and adding to the country's 1.2 million orphans.

I saw a group of people moving through the shantytown, engaging in what looked like a fraternity initiation. My teammate explained that it was a rite to observe a boy's movement into manhood.

Truth be told, it looked like most of these kids had already seen too much to be considered "kids" at all.

Soccer is an escape. You run and then you run some more, often more than 8 miles a game. You practice your skills until they're second nature—your feet, your body, your head become one with the ball.

But taking all those small steps with the ball is exhausting.

Sports have often led the way in breaking down barriers. Teams aren't based on color, language, or religion—they're grounded in competition, and the competitors couldn't care less about these distinctions.

No matter how skilled you are, the small steps you take with the ball won't be enough. Hold the ball too long, you're going to lose it. You can't do it yourself. You have to be able to pass the ball to your teammates.

My chance to play in a soccer match comes in an exhibition against Ajax's rival club, Vasco da Gama. My coach lets me play forward, and I get a couple of shots on goal. They either sail high over the net or fly straight into the keeper's arms.

The game is tied 0-0 at halftime. I'm dragging, totally exhausted. Normally, a liability on the field is an asset on the bench, but Coach has another idea: He sticks me in goal, where he hopes my deficiencies can stay hidden.

And for the most part they do, until one of Vasco's forwards manages to sneak one past me. Now we're losing, until one of my teammates picks up a goal to tie it. With a few seconds left in the game, another teammate draws a penalty. A free kick on goal.

"Dhani!" yells the coach. "You take the shot."

This time I know what to do. Don't aim high. Take what's there.

I keep the shot low. It goes in. We all hug in the middle of the field, having won the game.

Small steps.

RUNNING WITH THE BALL

Remember how people used to go running in those silver suits that were designed to make you overheat? The idea was that by working at a higher temperature, you'd work harder.

The small steps you have to take with a soccer ball have a similar effect. You have to slow down a little if you want to keep control of the ball. That slower pace helps you work on other aspects of running that you might not ordinarily focus on: balance, spatial awareness, proper footwork.

It's a great way to shore up your weaknesses without sacrificing your strengths.

Can't Fight Life

The original plan was India.

We weren't going to play cricket in Jamaica. When we sat down to plan the second season of *Dhani Tackles the Globe,* we were going to go to the heartland of cricket-crazy, the place where the sport has been tied into issues of politics, caste, and even religion for nearly 300 years.

Then Mumbai happened. A band of gunmen bombed, shot, and tortured their way through a series of hotels over 3 days, killing 173 people and wounding hundreds more.

Add to that the swine flu that was sweeping through Asia and Central America. Tsunamis ravaging Samoa. The threat of terrorism that has become part of our daily routine.

In simpler times, the scary part about travelling was getting there. Flight insurance was a popular part of many travel plans. Nowadays, you have to worry about death-and-dismemberment insurance for when you get there. Everybody carried a knife in Kingston, Jamaica. South Africa is one of the most violent places on the planet.

If you've got a modicum of celebrity—not to say I'm any kind of international superstar, but a lot of our visits were news enough for the local papers—you have to consider travelling with bodyguards, checking into hotels using aliases, and investing in kidnapping insurance. The worries don't end there. Do my bodyguards need to be strapped? Can I even trust the bodyguards? After all, many kidnappings are inside jobs.

Or am I overthinking everything?

The truth is, every time I step on a football field, I'm putting myself at risk of a career-ending injury—or worse, given everything we're finding out about concussions. But I can't think about any of that if I want to be sharp for the game.

We all have to live with the same basic fear: Is this the last day of life as we know it? Is a drunk driver going to plow through a red light into my car? Am I going to be hit by a stray bullet or a bolt of lightning? Is there an aneurysm in my heart that's about to explode?

And then we let it go.

Not everyone believes in a higher power, but I do. I believe in the powers-that-be, and I believe that they are looking out for me.

I'm not going to get kidnapped, because the powers-that-be want me to finish this show, to showcase this amazing country. They want me to be the guy who comes into a place, a face that the locals may not recognize, but that they get to know. When the next guy comes in, they've already seen somebody who looks like him, who talks like him, and maybe they're more inclined to embrace him.

The powers-that-be protect me when I'm playing sports. Maybe not always, but for as long as I'm supposed to be playing.

And once I accept that, I can let go. I'm just following the path that's laid out before me. Whatever happens is whatever happens.

People ask me, "Why do you do all this shit? Why do you go out there and get your ass kicked? Why are you putting yourself in harm's way?"

Because I'm supposed to!

Fantasy vs. Reality
(Mexico)

When I was a kid, Saturday was my favorite day. Not only could I sleep late, but when I woke up, wrestling was on.

I loved the characters. Hulk Hogan and Andre the Giant. Sergeant Slaughter and the Iron Sheik. Ted DiBiase, Tito Santana, Jimmy "Superfly" Snuka, and the Undertaker.

Then there were the moves: pile drivers, sleeper holds, figure-four leglocks, and my personal favorite, the leap from the top rope.

The action was only part of it. They wore hilarious costumes and participated in storylines. It was the perfect blend of sports and entertainment. Even as a kid, I knew these guys were acting. But they bled real blood, always leaving you wondering: What was real, and what was staged?

The kid inside me couldn't wait to get to Mexico City, where I was going to be spending a week doing *lucha libre,* the Mexican wrestling with the crazy masks.

I tried to focus on that Mexico City instead of the *other* Mexico City—the one with drug cartels, kidnappings, shootings, and beheadings.

On the one hand, a voice inside told me I was being paranoid. On the other, some of these stories were real. How the hell was I supposed to know which was which?

Lucha Libre

Professional wrestling started as entertainment, a popular attraction in sideshows and carnivals during the 19th century. In the 1930s, Salvador

Lutteroth Gonzales brought this style of entertainment back to his native Mexico, establishing the Empresa Mexicana de la Lucha Libre, the oldest surviving professional wrestling league in the world.

Lucha libre—Spanish for "free fighting"—quickly captured Mexico's imagination, making national heroes out of its stars. The most influential may have been "El Santo," a wrestler from the 1940s who entered the ring wearing a silver mask. The sense of mystery surrounding El Santo created many new fans and helped to elevate the sport to a whole new level of popularity. Before too long, masks became one of the most distinctive characteristics of lucha libre.

The lucha libre fighters are often more acrobatic than their American counterparts, who rely on size and power to defeat their opponents, but otherwise the sports are very similar. Each fighter tries to pin the other on the mat for 3 seconds or put him into a painful hold that forces him to submit.

And just like the American version, lucha libre trades in charismatic personalities and evolving storylines, usually a battle between good guys, or *técnicos*—skilled wrestlers who play by the rules—and *rudos,* the bad guys who cheat and behave in unsportsmanlike ways.

As with any good lucha libre match, mine had to begin with a story.

Shortly after arriving in Mexico City, I attended a fight with a couple of new friends, including a woman who was a professional wrestler herself. Like just about all the other fans, she was cursing like a sailor at the "villain," a masked wrestler who called himself Máscara Año 2000. When Máscara climbed over the ropes to continue bludgeoning his opponent outside the ring, my new friend continued to insult him.

Máscara seemed to be reaching a breaking point. He let go of the other wrestler and got into the woman's face, returning her insults.

So she tossed a full beer at him.

The situation escalated quickly from there. Máscara grabbed the woman by her lapels, clearly intending to do her harm.

It was up to Dhani Jones to save the day.

I jumped over the barrier that separated the fans from the wrestlers, grabbed Máscara, and put him into a headlock. I pushed him back toward the ring until we were separated by security guards.

The immediate danger defused, Máscara climbed back into the ring, picked up the microphone, and issued a challenge:

Come next Sunday, we would fight it out for real.

Whatever "real" means.

Later, Máscara and I held a prefight press conference, the kind you'll see the day before a boxing match. We took turns boasting about how each of us was going to dismantle the other. Then we stood up and stared each other down, putting on a performance for the cameras.

The nature of our show sometimes created a tension between fantasy and reality—the pursuit of the kind of drama that makes good television versus the fact that I was literally operating without a net.

Occasionally we blurred the line. In New Zealand, for example, my big moment came in an exhibition race specially arranged for the cameras. Other times I wore pads in situations where a legitimate participant might not have. My opponents in the various fights I've had weren't national champions, but fighters selected to match my often limited skill level.

But those fighters were still trying to kick my ass, sometimes even with an extra chip on their shoulder—for some of them, the chance to beat on someone they perceived as an American celebrity dilettante represented a real point of pride.

The lucha libre fight ratcheted this tension up to a whole new level. Sure, Máscara and I had staged the "grudge" in our upcoming grudge match. The fight would in many ways be more like a choreo-graphed dance, feigned brutality for the benefit of an audience and the cameras.

But a body slam is still a body slam. We weren't fighting on a mat-tress, but a semihard surface that rattled my bones every time I hit the ground. A surface that, after most matches, was mopped clean of blood. Real human blood. Stitches were common, as were knocked-out teeth and broken ribs.

I wasn't going to get myself killed in the ring, but I wasn't about to give the Bengals a heads-up about this particular episode, either. There was plenty of potential for the kind of injury that could put a crimp in my career. Or end it altogether.

Was I training for a fight or rehearsing for a show? I wasn't sure that I really knew the answer.

———————

And then there was Mexico City.

A place, from the stories I'd heard, where innocents were rou-tinely gunned down in the streets. Where the cops were in cahoots with the cartels. I'd seen the movie *Man on Fire,* fueling the idea that I could get kidnapped.

Crazy, right?

Or maybe not so crazy: My press conference with Máscara made the local papers—in a couple of cases, on the front page. People knew I was an American professional football player, and that American foot-ball players might be worth millions of dollars in ransom money. Sto-ries about the upcoming fight continued to run in the Mexico City newspapers every day I was there.

I wasn't the only person who considered the idea that I might be a target. I didn't have to ask for the bodyguards who accompanied us everywhere, or the convoys of SUVs that we used to travel the city. They were considered routine for a person with a public image.

I concentrated on the facts: Most kidnappings took place after weeks of surveillance. I was only going to be in Mexico City for a few days. I reminded myself that I was protected, both by the bodyguards and, I hoped, by a higher power.

Still, there were a couple of nights when I slept with a chair wedged against the door to make sure that no one could bust in.

Just in case.

POSTCARD FROM MEXICO CITY

Mexico City is a place with a turbulent history. It was founded by the Aztecs in the 14th century on an island in the middle of Lago de Texcoco, a lake some 7,300 feet above sea level, surrounded by higher mountains and plateaus. The Aztecs built an incredible series of dikes and canals to transform Texcoco into an area that they could actually farm.

Two hundred years later, Spanish visitors led by Hernán Cortés were so impressed by the Aztec improvements to the beautiful valley that they decided to conquer it.

Three hundred years after that, the locals revolted, establishing an independent Mexico.

But the real history of Mexico City begins in the 20th century. In 1900, the city was home to about half a million people. Today there are around 9 million, making it the third-largest city in the world and the largest metropolitan area in all of the Americas.

The growth hasn't been easy. While there is a great deal of wealth in the city, perhaps as much as 40 percent of the population lives in a state of poverty. Air pollution is an extreme problem—some estimate that 100,000 kids die every year as a result. Drug cartels play a major role in Mexican life, contributing to corruption in government and law enforcement and a murder rate nearly triple that of the United States.

But it's an extremely proud city. The Mexican colors fly everywhere. And while my preconceived notions of danger might have some basis in truth, daily life carries on in all the normal ways.

My guide in Mexico, Ignacio (a.k.a. "Nacho"), took me about 25 miles northeast of the city to Teotihuacán, where you can climb to the top of an ancient Aztec pyramid for an incredible view of the valley. We plodded up the 245 steps. It was just as amazing as Nacho had promised. He beamed with pride. "This is my country," he said.

Nacho wasn't a wrestler, but it would be hard to imagine a bigger fan of lucha libre. He was especially intrigued by the masks: He spent his days crafting silver jewelry depicting his favorites.

He explained to me that masks had been extremely important to the Aztecs. They used them to represent their gods, wearing them during important rituals in an attempt to harness supernatural powers.

The Aztec relationship to masks has carried into modern-day Mexico, but it has become slightly more complicated. The famous Mexican artist Frida Kahlo used them often in her paintings. The masks still represent an outward show of strength, the power of the gods. But they also create a sense of mystery, a persona, a chance to hide one's true self behind cover.

"Macho" is a Spanish word, and nowhere is that more evident than in Mexico City.

The favored drink is *mezcal,* which I discovered firsthand is not an easy drink to stomach. Drinkers prove their toughness by eating the worm at the bottom of the bottle.

Bull testicles, or *criadillas,* aren't just a delicacy, but are considered by many Mexican men to be a great source of virility and power.

Bullfights are still held every Sunday in an arena that seats 50,000, attracting people from all walks of life. Today's bullfighting is all about the show: The matador is at very little risk of losing to the bull, who is attacked by men on horseback with spears and poked with sharp sticks before his eventual executioner even enters the ring.

While it's framed as a test of manhood, it's more of a ritual sacrifice. I had trouble deciding if I was watching an exciting sporting event or a brutal display of animal cruelty.

"Machismo" means a display of "manly" characteristics. But does the display accurately represent the man?

———

Given the deep significance of masks in Mexican culture, it was no wonder that El Santo, the first *luchador* to don a mask, became such a national sensation—he was tapping into something deep in the Mexican consciousness.

Almost all luchadores wear masks as a symbol of their power. Having your mask ripped off during a fight is the ultimate humiliation. Sometimes masks are wagered between fighters to up the stakes of the fight. Some fighters refuse to ever appear in public without their masks.

I felt it was important to engage in this tradition, so I visited Sonora Market with Nacho. I tried on a series of masks, some of which were so terrifying that they scared me. I finally settled on a golden mask that gave me a name: Oro Sólido. Solid Gold.

———

I spent much of the week working out with Terry, a veteran luchador who had been fighting for over 30 years. It was an extremely acrobatic training, involving a lot of tumbling. Much of it was showmanship, like learning how to bounce off the ropes and leap over a charging opponent. But the most important aspects involved technique: the right way to slam an opponent to the ground and the best way to get slammed to the ground, while minimizing the damage to your body.

I wanted to learn more, like the dropkick—leaving the ground to fly feetfirst into an opponent. Or my favorite move from my days as a kid in front of the television: climbing to the top rope and dive-bombing my opponent from the air.

I was having fun, but I was still uncertain as to how to get my mind right. Should I be revving up for a fight or putting on a mask in preparation for a high school play?

Keeping in line with our recurring quest for a spiritual angle, I went to get a card reading. Mexico is predominantly Roman Catholic, but there are still vestiges of old superstitions and black magic. Reading tarot cards is part of that tradition.

I was a little nervous going in. Maybe I didn't want to know my fortune. Maybe the fortune-teller picked up on that.

"You're going to be fine," she said. "The fight will change your life if you believe in yourself."

I kind of laughed at the "believe in myself" part. Belief in myself isn't a quality that I usually lack.

But later, as I thought about it, it was a little more troubling.

When it came to this fight, who was I?

Social media is a mixed bag. In some ways, it has made love more vulnerable. There are more ways to check in, to diagnose situations without any conversation or context. "You've been on Facebook all day with God knows how many friends, you're twittering to God knows who, she texted me that he said that she said she saw you with her . . ."

But in other ways, that interconnectivity is a lifeline. I like to get on Facebook whenever I visit a new place, letting everyone know where I am. When I did that in Mexico City, I got an immediate reply from Gustavo, a friend of mine from high school: "You know I live down here, right?"

For a couple of nights, I ditched the crew and the show, hooking up with Gustavo and his friends. We went out to restaurants and bars. I even ventured out on my own, visiting clubs he recommended to me. The fact that the recommendations came from a friend created a sense of normalcy. I could finally connect with the city in a way that overcame my preconceptions. Mexico City wasn't a kidnapper's paradise with trouble around every corner; it was a real place with real people, real parties, and real life to be savored and experienced.

I entered the wrestling arena as Oro Sólido, hamming it up to the crowd, tossing flowers and gold coins to the fans.

I was ostensibly the good guy in this situation, the guy who had come to the defense of a woman. But I was also an outsider, a gringo come to engage in their sport after just 5 days of training.

Would national pride trump good and evil?

Hell yes, it would. There were 5-year-olds yelling at me who knew more curse words than I did. Old ladies screaming, "Fuck you, you stupid motherfucker!"

Outwardly I kept up my macho persona. But on the inside, I was feeling butterflies in my stomach. Were they prefight jitters or stage fright? I still couldn't tell.

A little voice in my head said: *What are you doing?*

Then the other voice chimed in: *Shut the hell up and we'll both find out.*

But I made a decision: When I got into the ring, I took off my mask. Whatever I was going to do next, I was going to do as me, not Oro Sólido.

"Me" reconnected with a sense of childhood joy. I was a wrestler, just like I used to watch on TV. I bounced off the ropes. I slammed and got slammed. And when the opportunity presented itself, I climbed up to the top rope and soared to the ground, landing on Máscara.

A few minutes later, I pinned him. The referee counted to three. I was the winner.

Or not quite: A few seconds later, the same referee disqualified me for supposedly kicking below the belt. The gringo could put on a good show, but it wasn't in the script for him to win. Mexican pride wouldn't allow it.

I didn't care. I was just happy to have been a part of the show, grinning like a kid on Saturday morning.

GET SKINNY

When it comes to physical movement, kids are born a little dumb. We were all toddlers once, tripping over things as we learned to walk, running into walls before we developed a sense of spatial relations.

Eventually we learn to move in a new way, whether by trial and error or through more directed activities like gymnastics and dancing. The kid who couldn't run three steps without stumbling is suddenly doing front flips off a lifeguard stand, sticking a perfect landing or rolling instinctively into a forward somersault.

By the time we're grown-ups, however, most of us have moved on from gymnastics and ballet. We forget what it's like to move as a kid. We've become more stable in our movements, but maybe a little more rigid as well.

My lucha libre training helped me to reconnect with that feeling of learning how to move again. When you flip or jump off the top rope, you have to be able to gauge where and how you're going to land. You always have to be in sync with the movements of your opponent—the fights aren't choreographed; they're about reacting and responding.

All the tumbling I did turned out to be great exercise for football. Not only was it helpful to practice falling down and getting up, but it reminded me of a concept that coaches will often call "getting skinny." They're not talking about losing weight, but about losing a mind-set: You don't always have to knock down the guy in front of you—sometimes it's about using grace and a sense of spatial relations to avoid contact altogether, finding a seam in the offensive line.

Ballet and gymnastics aren't just for little kids; they're for the grown adult who wants to know where he or she is at any moment in time. Dancing, stretching, and flexibility exercises are always going to enhance the overall experience of bodily health and wellness.

Connections

Why do we play sports, anyway?

It seems like an easy question, until you sit down and try to write a book about it.

I don't play for the exercise. I mean, the exercise is nice, but it's a lot easier to run on a treadmill than it is to scrounge up a bunch of people to play a game, let alone travel around the world to try to find one.

It's not for the paycheck. Maybe for some guys, but not me. I'll do all right by football when all's said and done, but probably not as well as I could have done as a pediatric neurosurgeon.

I think I play sports because it allows me to connect.

I connect to the kid inside of me. Wrestling in Switzerland or Mexico brings me back to my high school days. Italy puts me in touch with the joy of riding a bike all day. The surf lifesaving in Australia reminds me of my days as a competitive swimmer.

I connect to the me that I want to be. When I play volleyball in Brazil, I imagine I am Maverick from *Top Gun*. I joke a lot about wanting to be the first black James Bond, but I'm really only half-joking. I really want to be able to fly an airplane, jump out with a parachute into the ocean, and scuba dive to the entrance of the underwater tunnel. Blow up the gate, sneak inside, pick a lock, and fight a bunch of bad guys. When I take on multiple opponents practicing sambo in Russia or lift an Atlas Stone in Scotland, I feel like I'm on my way.

I connect to other people. One of the recurring jokes in the Bengals' locker room is that each area represents a 'hood. The guys with 1-year contracts are living in the projects. Sign a multiyear deal, you'll be moving on up to the estates. There's Rodeo Drive, Park Avenue, and the Country, Receiver Row, and the 'Hood. The team is a collection of incredibly different personalities from incredibly different backgrounds, some of whom I'd never have had the opportunity to meet, let alone develop a lifelong bond of friendship with. It's been even truer during my travels. I've built deep relationships, through competitive sport, with people who have never talked to a black man, let alone an NFL player.

Finally, sometimes I connect with powers that are larger than me. The world is a big place, and that's just the part we know. Playing sports helps me believe that there are spiritual forces that protect me, guide me, and, on occasion, teach me some of the most important lessons of my life.

Mountains Don't Lie
(Nepal)

I flew from Mexico City back to Cincinnati, but the turnaround wasn't long. Four days later, we were on a plane to Nepal, where I intended to climb to the top of Imja Tse, or Island Peak.

Over 20,300 feet high, Imja Tse was first climbed by a group that included the legendary Sherpa Tenzing Norgay, as a practice run for the ascent that he and Sir Edmund Hillary would make up Mount Everest a few weeks later.

On every previous episode of *Dhani Tackles the Globe*, I'd spent about a week to 10 days in each place. Nepal, however, came with its own set of special circumstances. It doesn't matter how great an athlete you are, you can't just sprint up the side of a mountain peak. Your body needs time to adjust to the increasing altitude, or, to put it bluntly, you will die in one of several unpleasant ways.

During my 1997 season at Michigan, Coach Carr gave everyone a copy of *Into Thin Air* as inspiration. It worked—we won the national championship—but the dangers of an Everest climb were still embedded in my mind.

Against the backdrop of this trip was the fact that the show had not yet been renewed for a new season. This might be the last episode, the Himalayan mountains our last stop.

But the Himalayas are anything but a "stop." You don't just drop in for a visit. You trek. And our trek was going to last 21 days.

MOUNTAINEERING

The oldest human mummy ever discovered wasn't in Egypt. It was Ötzi the Iceman, a 5,300-year-old man who was discovered in the Alps between Austria and Italy. There's a lot of evidence to suggest that Ötzi spent much of his life climbing up through the mountains. No one is sure why he chose to visit the specific peak where his body was found, but here's one man's guess:

Because it was there.

People have been tackling mountains for as long as there have been people. The Roman Emperor Hadrian went up Mount Etna in the year 121, supposedly to get a better view of the sunrise. Leonardo da Vinci climbed Mount Rosa, the highest peak in Switzerland, in the name of science. In 1857, a group of British gents met in London to form the Alpine Club. Their goal was to climb all the major peaks in Europe, an idea that was quickly replicated across the globe. Over the next 50 years, increasingly experienced mountaineers attempted to scale the world's highest peaks. While it never took off, "alpinism" was originally planned as an event in the Olympics' original charter in 1894.

Alpinism was considered the ultimate test of a man's mettle; generally a climber would carry what he needed on his back, clambering over rocks and ice to get to the top. The relatively isolated and much higher peaks of the Himalayas required mountaineers to shift to a more expeditionary approach: Getting to the mountain and acclimatizing oneself to the altitude could take days or weeks, so climbers began working in groups, enlisting porters to help carry the equipment. In 1953, Sir Edmund Hillary and Sherpa Tenzing Norgay used this approach to summit 29,029-foot Mount Everest, the world's tallest mountain.

By 1964, the world's tallest peaks had all been bagged. But mountaineering has become more popular than ever, especially as the art behind it continues to improve. Today's climbers have access to equipment, from crampons to oxygen tanks, that allows them to practice their sport with more safety and skill. In the first 40 years that the Himalayas were open to climbers, nearly 20,000 people made expeditions. Over the past 20 years, that number more than doubled.

But it's far from safe. Falling rocks and avalanches, surprise shifts in weather, exposure to solar radiation, and altitude sickness are among the dangers faced by these climbers. More than 1 in every 100 people who try to climb Mount Everest end up dead.

Why do people take the risk? The reasons are many. Some of them are trying to prove something to themselves. Others are just trying to commune with something larger than themselves at the places on earth that are closest to the heavens.

POSTCARD FROM NEPAL

No place on earth is quite like Nepal. At one extreme, along the border with India, the country is made up of tropical desert plains. At the other are the Himalayas, home to 8 of the 14 tallest mountains in the world.

The living conditions in Nepal seem just as extreme. Turbulent, often violent political battles over the future of the country continue today. Some estimates put the unemployment rate at around 50 percent. Poverty is everywhere; subsistence living is the norm.

The idea of suffering, however, is neither unfamiliar nor unbearable to the Nepalese. The vast majority of the people practice Hinduism, believing that we are born to suffer and to be reborn again, ultimately reaching moksha, *a spiritual release from all suffering. In a place closer to heaven than anywhere else, maybe they've got a point.*

We flew into Kathmandu, the only major city in Nepal, where I met Ang Ferba, the man who would be my Sherpa for the trip.

"Sherpa" is actually a family name describing a clan of people who emigrated from eastern Tibet to Nepal several hundred years ago. They are used to living at high altitudes and have accompanied nearly every expedition that has ever been attempted up Mount Everest. Ang himself was a veteran, having scaled Everest in 1979. He'd since retired from "serious" peaks, confessing that he didn't climb anything over 26,000 feet anymore. (In case you're wondering, 26,000 feet is still a mile higher than the tallest peak in North America.)

I was eager to get started, but first we took a class on the dangers of climbing. The real enemy wasn't the mountain, but the altitude. Several acronyms were thrown around: AMS (altitude mountain sickness), HACE (high altitude cerebral edema), HAPE (high altitude pulmonary edema). None of them sounded good. The instructor told us that, only a week ago, an experienced porter was found dead near one of the trails.

Like most Sherpas, Ang is a Buddhist. He took me to a monastery so that we could receive *puja,* a sacred blessing from a group of monks. I figured I could use all the help I could get.

Our Himalayan expedition, like most, began in Lukla, a village 9,350 feet above sea level where planes are able to land when the weather is right.

In addition to a Sherpa, most Himalayan expeditions involve porters, locals who literally carry the group's provisions on their backs. The scene was reminiscent of a group of workers outside Home Depot, dozens of potential porters lined up, looking to latch on to a trip. Ang selected a few whom he knew personally.

My body was already feeling the effects of the height. Fortunately we had a day to acclimate ourselves, and not much to do but sleep. Not like there were any clubs to go to. Lukla had a Starbucks, the last taste of the kind of civilization I'm accustomed to that I'd see for the next 3 weeks.

The journey really began at Sagarmatha National Park, where we walked through a ritual welcome gate, making sure to spin the prayer wheels along each side to secure the blessings of Chenrezig, the Buddhist god of compassion. A moment later we were treated to an absolutely incredible view of the terrain in front of us: enormous in scope, incredible in beauty.

After crossing a rickety suspension bridge, we walked about 2,000 feet straight up a hill. For Ang, the porters, and the donkeys who were carrying our gear, it was another day at the office. I was already exhausted. We finally made it to Namche Bazaar, elevation 11,200 feet, where once again Ang seemed to know everyone. Turned out he used to be the mayor.

A NOTE FROM JONATHAN FIERRO, PRODUCER

Usually we'd shoot 7 to 9 days. A day per segment, 6 or 7 per show. At the end of the day, you get to go to the hotel room. You get to have room service.

Nepal was 21 days. You shoot your bit, and guess what, Dhani? You can get some rice and potatoes. You get to sleep in a room with no heat, no electricity. The bathroom is a hole at the end of the hallway, or it's outside. There's no van to take you to work in the morning. There's no one waiting for you with fruit.

The deeper we got into the Himalayas, the more Sir Edmund Hillary's name seemed to pop up. I thought it was odd that the area's national hero was a guy from New Zealand, but Ang cleared up my confusion. After conquering Everest, Hillary founded the Himalayan Trust, a nonprofit organization dedicated to the place he'd fallen in love with. The trust has built hospitals, schools, forest nurseries, and bridges. I was reminded again that if there's anything better than the pleasure of accomplishing something, it's the pleasures of giving back to the people, communities, and world that helped you get where you needed to go.

We needed to go higher. Despite taking an extra day in each place to acclimate to the increasing altitude, every step was getting harder, not easier. Damn near impossible if I stopped to think about it, so I didn't—I just focused on keeping my head down, putting one foot in front of the other.

Every foot we climbed seemed to separate me from the world I was used to. Gone were the Internet cafés and familiar meals. Up here we ate what people had, which wasn't much—vegetables bled from the hardscrabble ground, yak meat with rice or pasta. Yak dung was treasured as a source of fuel for the fires that kept us warm; it was dried and stacked like logs in the rooms that doubled as outhouses. Human waste was recycled to help fertilize the agricultural soil.

We settled into a pattern: sleep, wake up, and go; sleep, wake up, and go. The same clothes every day. We were funky as all get-out. Extra, extra funky.

On the eighth day, we reached the snow line. I was also introduced to the first symptoms of altitude sickness: dizziness, headaches, a pressure behind my eyes. As tired as I was, sleeping was becoming a challenge, because breathing was becoming a challenge.

The main signal to your brain that it's time to breathe isn't a lack of oxygen, but a buildup of the carbon dioxide that you normally exhale. At higher altitudes, the lack of oxygen means you're producing less carbon dioxide, especially while you're sleeping. Lacking the appropriate trigger, your body forgets to breathe.

So my sleep was interrupted by what felt like a series of panic attacks. I'd wake up crying, pleading with my lungs to start working again.

I slept with my cell phone next to my head. It was the only way I knew to relieve the panic. I could text or call someone, connect with someone who was of the quote-unquote real world.

When the cell phone stopped working, I grabbed the satellite phone. But you had to go outside to use it, and it was so cold. Mostly I just slept near it, like a kid with a teddy bear, a reminder of a life that felt like a long time gone.

———

Above the tree line, the landscape started to look like desert. Ang kept reminding me to focus on what was in front of me. "Don't look up," he said. "Enjoy your walking, look down. When you look up, it feels more tiring." I concentrated on each step.

We passed a memorial to climbers who had died along the path we were travelling. Ang knew a few of them and stopped to pay respects. It was a reminder that death could be just around the corner.

As if my body wasn't already telling me the same thing.

The rest of the time, we walked. Just me, my backpack, and my friends. Nobody spoke much; we kind of entered our own separate spaces during the day.

Just walking. But that's what people did, right? They used to walk. There it is.

This is what life is all about.

You walk. You learn. You listen to your own heartbeat, breath, and the voice inside your head. You hear each step. You start to hear the environment around you in a way that you never would back home.

Just walking.

———

We reached Everest base camp at over 18,000 feet. The night sky was intense: With no light pollution, you could see the Milky Way the way our ancestors did, full of stories, mysteries, and possibilities.

The daytime was a different story. Every time I looked up, the mountains seemed farther away. My heart beat faster. Breathing got harder. My tongue kept getting stuck to the roof of my mouth, requiring water to pry it off. I'd stop every five steps to allow my oxygen-deprived brain to engage in the same repetitive debate: *You don't have to do this.*

Each time I'd start again. Somehow I made the steep climb up Kala Pattar, where I had an unobstructed, amazing view of Mount Everest. Another 2,000 feet of climbing and we'd reach our goal, Island Peak.

Except that I wasn't going to make it. I had to get out of there. I knew it was time to go home.

A NOTE FROM JONATHAN FIERRO, PRODUCER

Dhani pulled me aside and was like, "I'm done. My legs are shot. I don't have it." We had one more peak to go. It was the only time in the history of the show he ever said no.

I respect that. He knows his body a lot better than I do.

"Cool," I said. "But I'm producing a show, and we lost our last element. I'm going to have to show you as if you quit or failed."

Dhani wasn't happy about that. But he was okay with it.

I was physically exhausted, but my brain was racing. Last episode of the show and I am going to fail. And everyone's going to get to see me fail on television.

Forget about all that. My body is more important than any show. And my body is . . .

Done.

But the story wasn't over yet.

On the way down Kala Pattar, we passed a fallen hiker, a 67-year-old Belgian man who had succumbed to altitude sickness.

He wasn't dead, but he was on his way. I stood back and watched the Sherpas work on the guy, massaging his arms and legs. They picked him up like they were going to carry him down the hill, only to put him down again.

There's something wrong, I thought. *This is taking too long.* I watched the guides pick up the hiker and put him down a second time. *That's it. Next time they put him down, I'm taking him.*

When they put the hiker down for a third time, I stepped in. "Let me do this," I told them.

I put the hiker onto my shoulders. The Sherpas flanked me, keeping me steady as I made my way down the hill.

I wasn't thinking about me anymore, about what I could or couldn't do, about how exhausted I was, how little oxygen my body was receiving.

It was, by far, the easiest part of the journey.

Thirty minutes later, we arrived back at the lodge. The hiker was taken by helicopter to a hospital, where he was revived and returned to health.

Altitude Training

Athletes use altitude training all the time to encourage their bodies to become less dependent on oxygen. The science is simple: Get back to a place where there's more oxygen, and you're going to feel like Superman.

The key is not to overdo it. There's a point at which your body starts breaking down, eliminating any gains you might have hoped to achieve. But if your gym has an altitude chamber, give it a go.

Or better yet, go climb a mountain.

A Note from Don Yee, Agent

I think at some point Dhani decided, "It has nothing to do with me."

That's hard for a lot of guys. It feels like a loss of control. Whatever it is about him that allowed him to identify a need for a plan of action that included "Maybe I need to listen to this other person who may have a different vision for me than I have for myself," I think that it's something that he deserves tremendous credit for. A lot of players get jaded, and they don't allow themselves to listen. They get straitjacketed mentally.

But Dhani didn't. In fact, I've only seen him continue to grow and become even more grounded. I think he has several more good years of football ahead. Which is a huge credit to him, because at the time he came to me a lot of people thought he might be done.

Physically, right now, he's just as good as he's ever been. His leadership qualities and his ability to nurture young players are going to be big benefits to him. But it's the growth, tremendous personal growth—I'm really proud of him.

The 11th Floor

I came back from Nepal a little broken.

I was surprised at how hard the environment was.

How hard the world is.

We learned shortly after our return that the show was over—there would be no third season of *Dhani Tackles the Globe*. It seemed somehow appropriate that the hardest show would be the last.

Despite his threats on the mountain, Jonathan didn't cut the episode in a way that emphasized my failure to reach the last peak. He opted for the storybook ending, me carrying the fallen hiker down the hill.

But for a while, I found myself wishing that I had done more. I wanted to be able to say to myself, "Man, you really got everything out of the experience that you could have." I wished that I could have appreciated it more while I was there. To have experienced, with a little more depth and gratitude, that fleeting sense of connection to the forces much larger than we are.

Nepal had been the most enduring adventure I've ever embarked upon. It was a hellish experience that, in some capacity, I wish no one to do, yet I want everybody to experience.

Yes, I came back a little broken. But I think I came back stronger, too.

Maybe you are meant to experience the journey in the way that you did in the moment that you did it. It wasn't up to you to say that you didn't get what you needed, because whatever you needed, you definitely got—just not in the way that you may have wished, or in the way that you thought you would receive it.

Maybe this was an opportunity for self-evaluation. To realize that not all things are for you. Maybe there are boundaries, certain places or things that you shouldn't do. Or things that you should do, but are a little bit more challenging than you would have expected. Maybe doing them will make you stronger, wiser, or more in touch with the world around you.

Maybe you are more dependent upon more things than you thought. Maybe you can be more independent.

Or maybe you don't have to be. Maybe it's okay to depend on the people in our lives, our beliefs in the mysterious forces that are outside our comprehension or control. Maybe it's okay to believe in the world.

It's hard to imagine a better teacher.

I still remember putting those stakes in the ground, building that tent, so no matter what happened, I'd still be able to build my foundation. Then the first floor. Second floor.

Now I'm on the 11th floor of my skyscraper. When I look down, I can see the places where I changed contractors, altering the shape or design of the building.

I don't have any idea how many floors there will be. That part's not up to me. But the view keeps getting better.

I can see how the world is connected in ways, I'd never imagined. A Red Stripe ad in Scotland promoting the lifestyle I'd experience a few days later in Jamaica. Pradal Serey gives rise to Muay Thai, which helps shape Russian Sambo. Mandela and his fellow South African apartheid fighters used soccer in the same way that medieval Irish parishes used hurling—not just to compete, but to connect. Not just to best one's fellow man, but to better him.

No matter how high it gets, I'm never going to shut myself in. My building is only one of many. If I want to keep growing, I've got to keep getting out there, seeing and experiencing what there is to see.

Where the punches are real punches. The sharks are real sharks. The mountains are real mountains.

I hope to see you there.

Acknowledgments

The author would simply like to thank his family, the one he was born with and the members he's acquired along the way.